This Migraine Journal
Belongs To:

_____

Kick Those
Headaches In
The Membrain!

| Mon | Tue | Wed | Thu | Fri | Sat | Sun | Date: | Temp: |

Locations of Pain:

Weather Outside:

Notes:

Pain Tolerance Level:

Triggers:

Eye Strain.....................
Bright Lights................
Loud Sounds...............
Strong Smells.............
Home Stress................
Driving Stress..............
Work Stress.................
Caffeine.......................
Alcohol........................
Hunger........................
Food Choice...............
Oversleep....................
Lack of Sleep.............
Illness..........................
Allergies......................
Exertion.......................
Dehydration................
Blood Pressure...........
PMS..............................

Pain Relief Methods Tried:

Medications Used:

Daily Routine Changes:

Additional Notes:

| Begin Time: | End Time: | Duration: |

Suggestions For Next Time:

| Mon | Tue | Wed | Thu | Fri | Sat | Sun | Date: | Temp: |

Locations of Pain:

Weather
Outside:

Notes:

Pain Tolerance Level:

Triggers:

Eye Strain.................
Bright Lights.............
Loud Sounds.............
Strong Smells...........
Home Stress.............
Driving Stress...........
Work Stress..............
Caffeine....................
Alcohol......................
Hunger......................
Food Choice.............
Oversleep.................
Lack of Sleep...........
Illness.......................
Allergies....................
Exertion....................
Dehydration..............
Blood Pressure.........
PMS...........................

Pain Relief
Methods Tried:

Medications
Used:

Daily Routine
Changes:

Additional Notes:

Begin
Time:

End
Time:

Duration:

Suggestions
For Next Time:

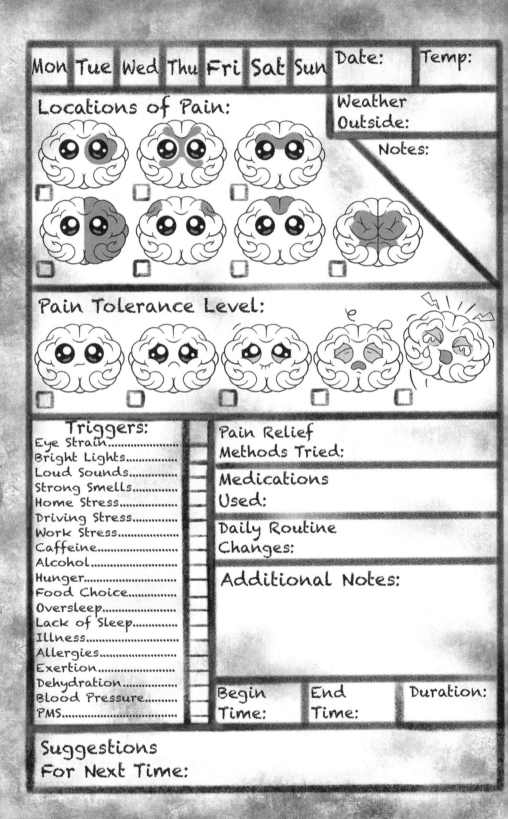

| Mon | Tue | Wed | Thu | Fri | Sat | Sun | Date: | Temp: |

Locations of Pain:

Weather Outside:

Notes:

Pain Tolerance Level:

Triggers:
Eye Strain...............
Bright Lights..............
Loud Sounds...............
Strong Smells..............
Home Stress...............
Driving Stress..............
Work Stress...............
Caffeine....................
Alcohol....................
Hunger.....................
Food Choice...............
Oversleep...................
Lack of Sleep.............
Illness.....................
Allergies..................
Exertion...................
Dehydration...............
Blood Pressure...........
PMS.......................

Pain Relief Methods Tried:

Medications Used:

Daily Routine Changes:

Additional Notes:

Begin Time:

End Time:

Duration:

Suggestions For Next Time:

Mon	Tue	Wed	Thu	Fri	Sat	Sun	Date:	Temp:

Locations of Pain:

Weather
Outside:

Notes:

Pain Tolerance Level:

Triggers:
Eye Strain........................
Bright Lights..................
Loud Sounds..................
Strong Smells................
Home Stress....................
Driving Stress................
Work Stress....................
Caffeine............................
Alcohol.............................
Hunger.............................
Food Choice...................
Oversleep.........................
Lack of Sleep.................
Illness................................
Allergies...........................
Exertion...........................
Dehydration...................
Blood Pressure.............
PMS....................................

Pain Relief
Methods Tried:

Medications
Used:

Daily Routine
Changes:

Additional Notes:

Begin Time:	End Time:	Duration:

Suggestions For Next Time:

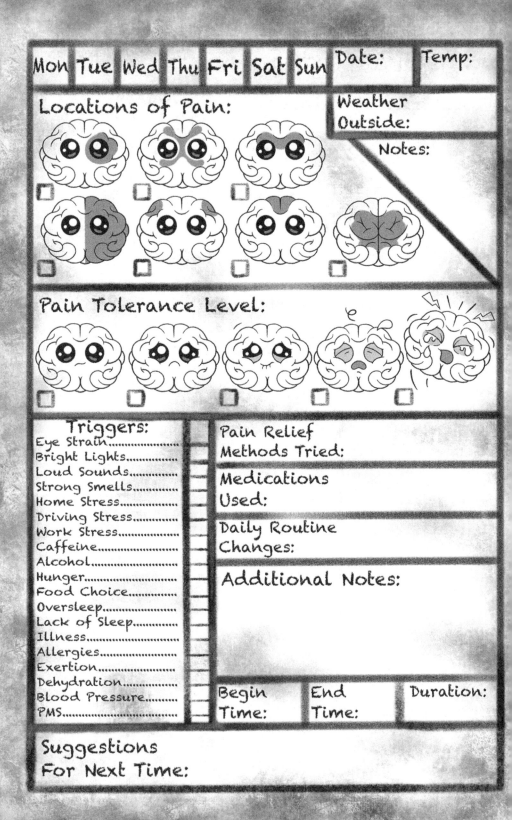

| Mon | Tue | Wed | Thu | Fri | Sat | Sun | Date: | | Temp: |

Locations of Pain:

Weather
Outside:

Notes:

Pain Tolerance Level:

Triggers:
Eye Strain......................
Bright Lights................
Loud Sounds...............
Strong Smells..............
Home Stress................
Driving Stress..............
Work Stress.................
Caffeine........................
Alcohol.........................
Hunger.........................
Food Choice...............
Oversleep.....................
Lack of Sleep.............
Illness..........................
Allergies......................
Exertion.......................
Dehydration...............
Blood Pressure..........
PMS...............................

Pain Relief
Methods Tried:

Medications
Used:

Daily Routine
Changes:

Additional Notes:

Begin
Time:

End
Time:

Duration:

Suggestions
For Next Time:

Mon | Tue | Wed | Thu | Fri | Sat | Sun

Date:

Temp:

Locations of Pain:

Weather Outside:

Notes:

Pain Tolerance Level:

Triggers:

Eye Strain..........................
Bright Lights......................
Loud Sounds.....................
Strong Smells....................
Home Stress......................
Driving Stress...................
Work Stress......................
Caffeine...........................
Alcohol.............................
Hunger..............................
Food Choice......................
Oversleep..........................
Lack of Sleep...................
Illness...............................
Allergies...........................
Exertion.............................
Dehydration.......................
Blood Pressure..................
PMS..................................

Pain Relief Methods Tried:

Medications Used:

Daily Routine Changes:

Additional Notes:

Begin Time:

End Time:

Duration:

Suggestions For Next Time:

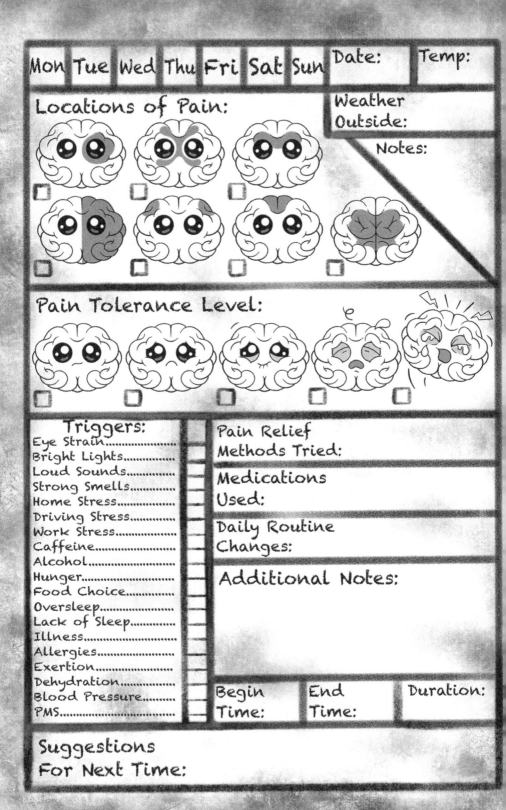

| Mon | Tue | Wed | Thu | Fri | Sat | Sun | Date: | Temp: |

Locations of Pain:

Weather Outside:

Notes:

Pain Tolerance Level:

Triggers:

Eye Strain......................
Bright Lights................
Loud Sounds................
Strong Smells..............
Home Stress................
Driving Stress..............
Work Stress..................
Caffeine..........................
Alcohol............................
Hunger............................
Food Choice................
Oversleep......................
Lack of Sleep..............
Illness..............................
Allergies........................
Exertion..........................
Dehydration..................
Blood Pressure............
PMS..................................

Pain Relief Methods Tried:

Medications Used:

Daily Routine Changes:

Additional Notes:

Begin Time:

End Time:

Duration:

Suggestions For Next Time:

| Mon | Tue | Wed | Thu | Fri | Sat | Sun | Date: | Temp: |

Locations of Pain:

Weather Outside:

Notes:

Pain Tolerance Level:

Triggers:

Eye Strain.....................
Bright Lights................
Loud Sounds...............
Strong Smells..............
Home Stress................
Driving Stress..............
Work Stress.................
Caffeine.......................
Alcohol........................
Hunger........................
Food Choice...............
Oversleep....................
Lack of Sleep.............
Illness.........................
Allergies......................
Exertion......................
Dehydration................
Blood Pressure..........
PMS.............................

Pain Relief Methods Tried:

Medications Used:

Daily Routine Changes:

Additional Notes:

| Begin Time: | End Time: | Duration: |

Suggestions For Next Time:

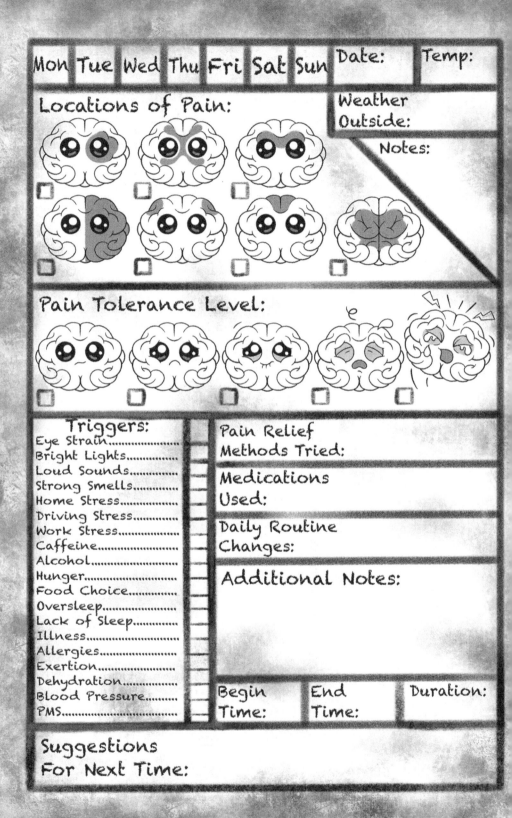

Mon Tue Wed Thu Fri Sat Sun   Date: Temp:

Locations of Pain:

Weather
Outside:

Notes:

Pain Tolerance Level:

Triggers:
Eye Strain...............
Bright Lights...............
Loud Sounds...............
Strong Smells...............
Home Stress...............
Driving Stress...............
Work Stress...............
Caffeine...............
Alcohol...............
Hunger...............
Food Choice...............
Oversleep...............
Lack of Sleep...............
Illness...............
Allergies...............
Exertion...............
Dehydration...............
Blood Pressure...........
PMS...............

Pain Relief
Methods Tried:

Medications
Used:

Daily Routine
Changes:

Additional Notes:

Begin
Time:

End
Time:

Duration:

Suggestions
For Next Time:

| Mon | Tue | Wed | Thu | Fri | Sat | Sun | Date: | Temp: |

Locations of Pain:

Weather Outside:

Notes:

Pain Tolerance Level:

Triggers:
Eye Strain...............
Bright Lights...............
Loud Sounds...............
Strong Smells...............
Home Stress...............
Driving Stress...............
Work Stress...............
Caffeine...............
Alcohol...............
Hunger...............
Food Choice...............
Oversleep...............
Lack of Sleep...............
Illness...............
Allergies...............
Exertion...............
Dehydration...............
Blood Pressure...............
PMS...............

Pain Relief Methods Tried:

Medications Used:

Daily Routine Changes:

Additional Notes:

Begin Time:

End Time:

Duration:

Suggestions For Next Time:

| Mon | Tue | Wed | Thu | Fri | Sat | Sun | Date: | Temp: |

Locations of Pain:

Weather Outside:

Notes:

Pain Tolerance Level:

Triggers:

Eye Strain...............
Bright Lights...............
Loud Sounds...............
Strong Smells...............
Home Stress...............
Driving Stress...............
Work Stress...............
Caffeine...............
Alcohol...............
Hunger...............
Food Choice...............
Oversleep...............
Lack of Sleep...............
Illness...............
Allergies...............
Exertion...............
Dehydration...............
Blood Pressure...............
PMS...............

Pain Relief Methods Tried:

Medications Used:

Daily Routine Changes:

Additional Notes:

Begin Time:

End Time:

Duration:

Suggestions For Next Time:

Mon | Tue | Wed | Thu | Fri | Sat | Sun   Date: Temp:

Locations of Pain:
Weather
Outside:
Notes:

☐ ☐ ☐
☐ ☐ ☐ ☐

Pain Tolerance Level:
☐ ☐ ☐ ☐ ☐

Triggers:
Eye Strain.................
Bright Lights.............
Loud Sounds.............
Strong Smells...........
Home Stress.............
Driving Stress...........
Work Stress..............
Caffeine...................
Alcohol.....................
Hunger.....................
Food Choice.............
Oversleep.................
Lack of Sleep............
Illness......................
Allergies...................
Exertion....................
Dehydration..............
Blood Pressure..........
PMS..........................

Pain Relief
Methods Tried:

Medications
Used:

Daily Routine
Changes:

Additional Notes:

Begin
Time: End
Time: Duration:

Suggestions
For Next Time:

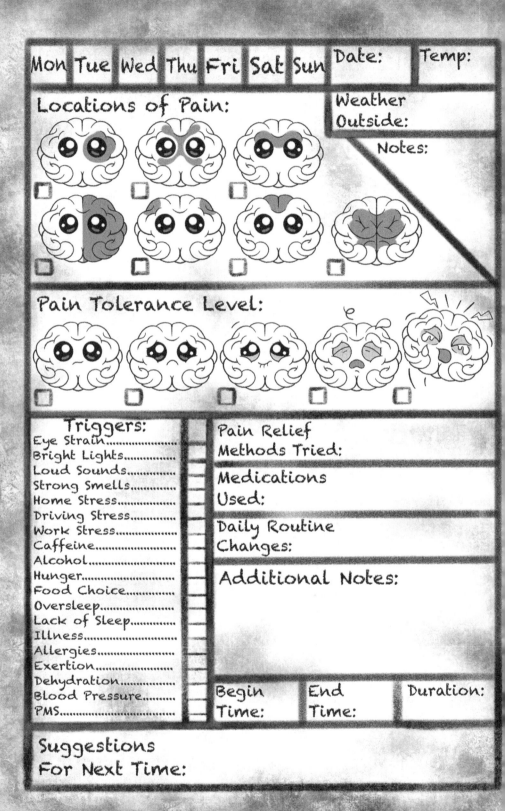

| Mon | Tue | Wed | Thu | Fri | Sat | Sun | Date: | Temp: |

Locations of Pain:

Weather
Outside:

Notes:

Pain Tolerance Level:

Triggers:
Eye Strain.................
Bright Lights..............
Loud Sounds..............
Strong Smells............
Home Stress..............
Driving Stress............
Work Stress..............
Caffeine....................
Alcohol.....................
Hunger......................
Food Choice..............
Oversleep..................
Lack of Sleep.............
Illness......................
Allergies...................
Exertion....................
Dehydration..............
Blood Pressure..........
PMS.........................

Pain Relief
Methods Tried:

Medications
Used:

Daily Routine
Changes:

Additional Notes:

Begin
Time:

End
Time:

Duration:

Suggestions
For Next Time:

| Mon | Tue | Wed | Thu | Fri | Sat | Sun | Date: | Temp: |

Locations of Pain:

Weather Outside:

Notes:

Pain Tolerance Level:

Triggers:

Eye Strain.......................
Bright Lights................
Loud Sounds...............
Strong Smells................
Home Stress..................
Driving Stress.................
Work Stress....................
Caffeine............................
Alcohol.............................
Hunger............................
Food Choice...............
Oversleep......................
Lack of Sleep.............
Illness..............................
Allergies..........................
Exertion...........................
Dehydration................
Blood Pressure..........
PMS...................................

Pain Relief Methods Tried:

Medications Used:

Daily Routine Changes:

Additional Notes:

Begin Time: | End Time: | Duration:

Suggestions For Next Time:

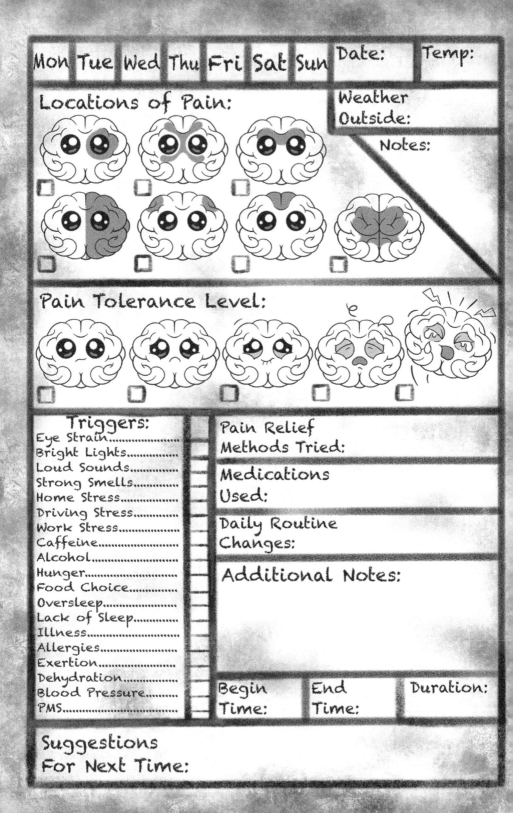

| Mon | Tue | Wed | Thu | Fri | Sat | Sun | Date: | Temp: |

Locations of Pain:

Weather Outside:

Notes:

Pain Tolerance Level:

Triggers:

Eye Strain...............
Bright Lights.............
Loud Sounds...........
Strong Smells...........
Home Stress.............
Driving Stress...........
Work Stress.............
Caffeine.................
Alcohol.................
Hunger.................
Food Choice............
Oversleep...............
Lack of Sleep...........
Illness.................
Allergies...............
Exertion...............
Dehydration............
Blood Pressure..........
PMS...................

Pain Relief Methods Tried:

Medications Used:

Daily Routine Changes:

Additional Notes:

Begin Time:

End Time:

Duration:

Suggestions For Next Time:

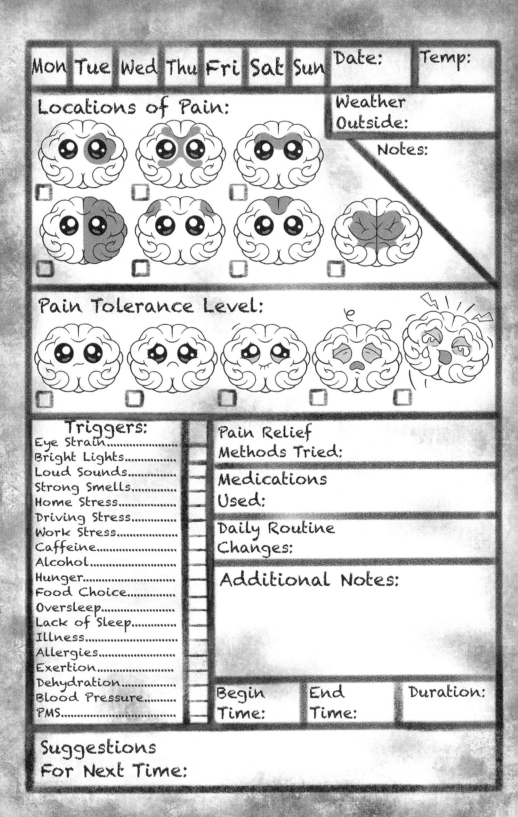

Mon Tue Wed Thu Fri Sat Sun   Date: Temp:

Locations of Pain:

Weather Outside:

Notes:

Pain Tolerance Level:

Triggers:
Eye Strain..................
Bright Lights..............
Loud Sounds..............
Strong Smells...........
Home Stress.............
Driving Stress...........
Work Stress..............
Caffeine....................
Alcohol.....................
Hunger......................
Food Choice.............
Oversleep..................
Lack of Sleep............
Illness.......................
Allergies....................
Exertion....................
Dehydration..............
Blood Pressure..........
PMS..........................

Pain Relief Methods Tried:

Medications Used:

Daily Routine Changes:

Additional Notes:

Begin Time: End Time: Duration:

Suggestions For Next Time:

Mon	Tue	Wed	Thu	Fri	Sat	Sun	Date:	Temp:

Locations of Pain:

Weather
Outside:

Notes:

Pain Tolerance Level:

Triggers:

Eye Strain....................
Bright Lights................
Loud Sounds................
Strong Smells...............
Home Stress.................
Driving Stress...............
Work Stress..................
Caffeine.......................
Alcohol........................
Hunger........................
Food Choice.................
Oversleep....................
Lack of Sleep...............
Illness.........................
Allergies......................
Exertion.......................
Dehydration.................
Blood Pressure............
PMS............................

Pain Relief
Methods Tried:

Medications
Used:

Daily Routine
Changes:

Additional Notes:

Begin Time:	End Time:	Duration:

Suggestions
For Next Time:

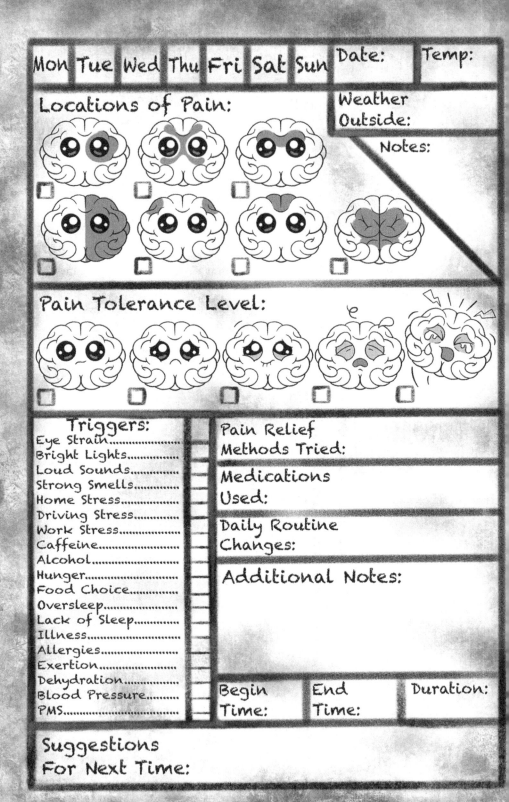

Mon | Tue | Wed | Thu | Fri | Sat | Sun

Date:

Temp:

Locations of Pain:

Weather Outside:

Notes:

Pain Tolerance Level:

Triggers:
Eye Strain.........................
Bright Lights...................
Loud Sounds....................
Strong Smells..................
Home Stress.....................
Driving Stress.................
Work Stress......................
Caffeine............................
Alcohol.............................
Hunger..............................
Food Choice.....................
Oversleep.........................
Lack of Sleep..................
Illness..............................
Allergies...........................
Exertion............................
Dehydration.....................
Blood Pressure...............
PMS....................................

Pain Relief
Methods Tried:

Medications
Used:

Daily Routine
Changes:

Additional Notes:

Begin
Time:

End
Time:

Duration:

Suggestions
For Next Time:

Mon Tue Wed Thu Fri Sat Sun

Date:

Temp:

Locations of Pain:

Weather
Outside:

Notes:

Pain Tolerance Level:

Triggers:

Eye Strain.....................
Bright Lights................
Loud Sounds................
Strong Smells..............
Home Stress.................
Driving Stress..............
Work Stress..................
Caffeine.......................
Alcohol.........................
Hunger..........................
Food Choice................
Oversleep......................
Lack of Sleep..............
Illness..........................
Allergies.......................
Exertion.......................
Dehydration..................
Blood Pressure............
PMS..............................

Pain Relief
Methods Tried:

Medications
Used:

Daily Routine
Changes:

Additional Notes:

Begin
Time:

End
Time:

Duration:

Suggestions
For Next Time:

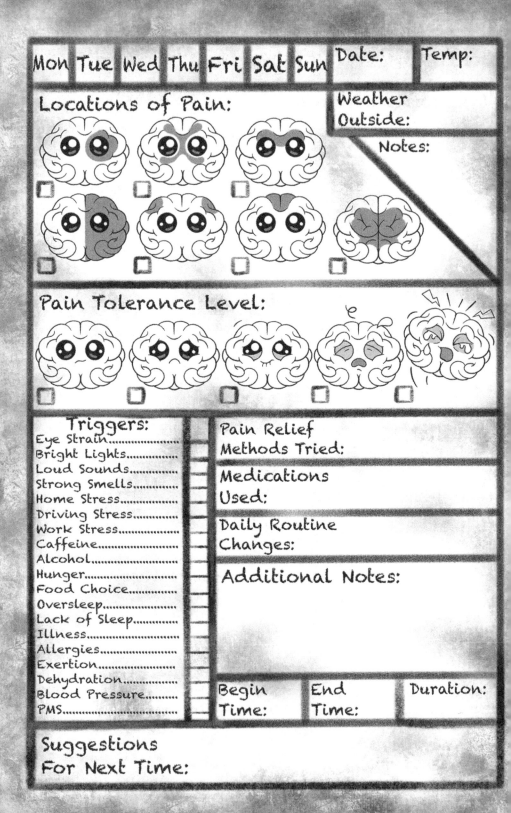

| Mon | Tue | Wed | Thu | Fri | Sat | Sun | Date: | Temp: |

Locations of Pain:

Weather Outside:

Notes:

Pain Tolerance Level:

Triggers:

Eye Strain...................
Bright Lights...............
Loud Sounds...............
Strong Smells.............
Home Stress...............
Driving Stress.............
Work Stress................
Caffeine.......................
Alcohol.........................
Hunger.........................
Food Choice...............
Oversleep....................
Lack of Sleep..............
Illness..........................
Allergies......................
Exertion.......................
Dehydration................
Blood Pressure...........
PMS..............................

Pain Relief Methods Tried:

Medications Used:

Daily Routine Changes:

Additional Notes:

Begin Time:

End Time:

Duration:

Suggestions For Next Time:

Mon Tue Wed Thu Fri Sat Sun

Date:

Temp:

Locations of Pain:

Weather Outside:

Notes:

Pain Tolerance Level:

Triggers:
Eye Strain...................
Bright Lights...............
Loud Sounds................
Strong Smells..............
Home Stress................
Driving Stress.............
Work Stress.................
Caffeine.......................
Alcohol........................
Hunger.........................
Food Choice................
Oversleep.....................
Lack of Sleep..............
Illness.........................
Allergies.....................
Exertion......................
Dehydration................
Blood Pressure..........
PMS.............................

Pain Relief Methods Tried:

Medications Used:

Daily Routine Changes:

Additional Notes:

Begin Time:

End Time:

Duration:

Suggestions For Next Time:

| Mon | Tue | Wed | Thu | Fri | Sat | Sun | Date: | Temp: |

Locations of Pain:

Weather
Outside:

Notes:

Pain Tolerance Level:

Triggers:
Eye Strain..............
Bright Lights..............
Loud Sounds..............
Strong Smells..............
Home Stress..............
Driving Stress..............
Work Stress..............
Caffeine..............
Alcohol..............
Hunger..............
Food Choice..............
Oversleep..............
Lack of Sleep..............
Illness..............
Allergies..............
Exertion..............
Dehydration..............
Blood Pressure..........
PMS..............

Pain Relief
Methods Tried:

Medications
Used:

Daily Routine
Changes:

Additional Notes:

Begin
Time:

End
Time:

Duration:

Suggestions
For Next Time:

| Mon | Tue | Wed | Thu | Fri | Sat | Sun | Date: | Temp: |

Locations of Pain:

Weather Outside:

Notes:

Pain Tolerance Level:

Triggers:
Eye Strain...............
Bright Lights.................
Loud Sounds................
Strong Smells..............
Home Stress................
Driving Stress............
Work Stress................
Caffeine.......................
Alcohol.........................
Hunger.........................
Food Choice...............
Oversleep.....................
Lack of Sleep.............
Illness...........................
Allergies.......................
Exertion.......................
Dehydration................
Blood Pressure..........
PMS...............................

Pain Relief Methods Tried:

Medications Used:

Daily Routine Changes:

Additional Notes:

Begin Time:

End Time:

Duration:

Suggestions For Next Time:

| Mon | Tue | Wed | Thu | Fri | Sat | Sun | Date: | Temp: |

Locations of Pain:

Weather
Outside:

Notes:

Pain Tolerance Level:

Triggers:

Eye Strain..........................
Bright Lights....................
Loud Sounds.................
Strong Smells.................
Home Stress....................
Driving Stress.............
Work Stress....................
Caffeine............................
Alcohol.............................
Hunger...............................
Food Choice.................
Oversleep........................
Lack of Sleep............
Illness..............................
Allergies.........................
Exertion..........................
Dehydration..................
Blood Pressure...........
PMS......................................

Pain Relief
Methods Tried:

Medications
Used:

Daily Routine
Changes:

Additional Notes:

Begin
Time:

End
Time:

Duration:

Suggestions
For Next Time:

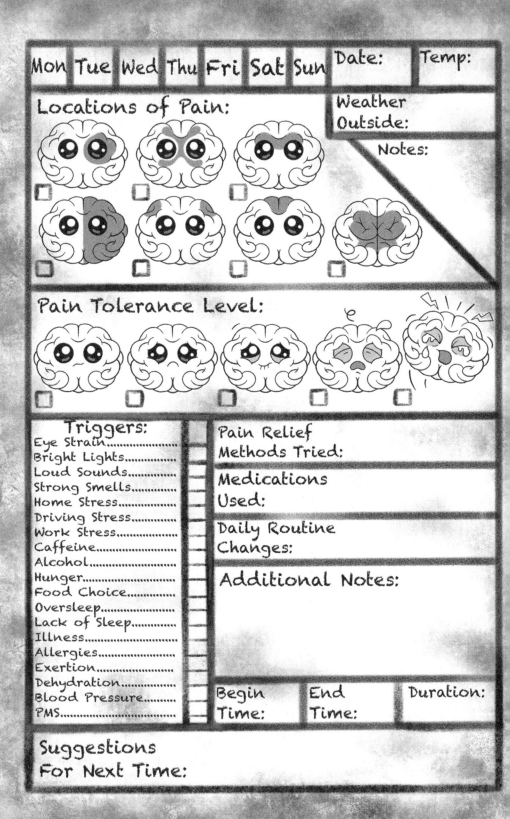

Mon | Tue | Wed | Thu | Fri | Sat | Sun | Date: | Temp:

Weather Outside:

Locations of Pain:

Notes:

Pain Tolerance Level:

Triggers:
Eye Strain.................
Bright Lights.............
Loud Sounds.............
Strong Smells...........
Home Stress..............
Driving Stress...........
Work Stress...............
Caffeine....................
Alcohol......................
Hunger......................
Food Choice.............
Oversleep..................
Lack of Sleep............
Illness.......................
Allergies....................
Exertion....................
Dehydration..............
Blood Pressure.........
PMS...........................

Pain Relief Methods Tried:

Medications Used:

Daily Routine Changes:

Additional Notes:

Begin Time: | End Time: | Duration:

Suggestions For Next Time:

Mon Tue Wed Thu Fri Sat Sun   Date: Temp:

Locations of Pain:

Weather
Outside:

Notes:

Pain Tolerance Level:

Triggers:
Eye Strain.................
Bright Lights.................
Loud Sounds.................
Strong Smells.................
Home Stress.................
Driving Stress.................
Work Stress.................
Caffeine.................
Alcohol.................
Hunger.................
Food Choice.................
Oversleep.................
Lack of Sleep.................
Illness.................
Allergies.................
Exertion.................
Dehydration.................
Blood Pressure.................
PMS.................

Pain Relief
Methods Tried:

Medications
Used:

Daily Routine
Changes:

Additional Notes:

Begin
Time:

End
Time:

Duration:

Suggestions
For Next Time:

| Mon | Tue | Wed | Thu | Fri | Sat | Sun | Date: | Temp: |

Locations of Pain:

Weather
Outside:

Notes:

☐ ☐ ☐

☐ ☐ ☐ ☐

Pain Tolerance Level:

☐ ☐ ☐ ☐ ☐

Triggers:

Eye Strain...............
Bright Lights.................
Loud Sounds................
Strong Smells.................
Home Stress..................
Driving Stress..............
Work Stress.................
Caffeine......................
Alcohol.........................
Hunger........................
Food Choice..................
Oversleep.....................
Lack of Sleep..............
Illness..........................
Allergies......................
Exertion.......................
Dehydration.................
Blood Pressure..........
PMS..............................

Pain Relief
Methods Tried:

Medications
Used:

Daily Routine
Changes:

Additional Notes:

| Begin Time: | End Time: | Duration: |

Suggestions For Next Time:

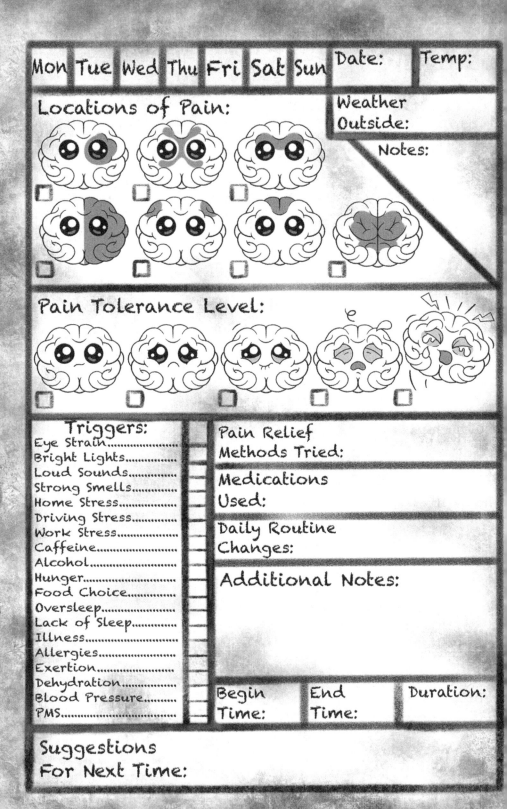

| Mon | Tue | Wed | Thu | Fri | Sat | Sun | Date: | Temp: |

Locations of Pain:

Weather
Outside:

Notes:

☐ ☐ ☐

☐ ☐ ☐ ☐

Pain Tolerance Level:

☐ ☐ ☐ ☐ ☐

Triggers:

Eye Strain.....................
Bright Lights.................
Loud Sounds................
Strong Smells..............
Home Stress.................
Driving Stress..............
Work Stress..................
Caffeine........................
Alcohol.........................
Hunger..........................
Food Choice.................
Oversleep......................
Lack of Sleep..............
Illness...........................
Allergies.......................
Exertion........................
Dehydration.................
Blood Pressure...........
PMS..............................

Pain Relief
Methods Tried:

Medications
Used:

Daily Routine
Changes:

Additional Notes:

Begin
Time:

End
Time:

Duration:

Suggestions
For Next Time:

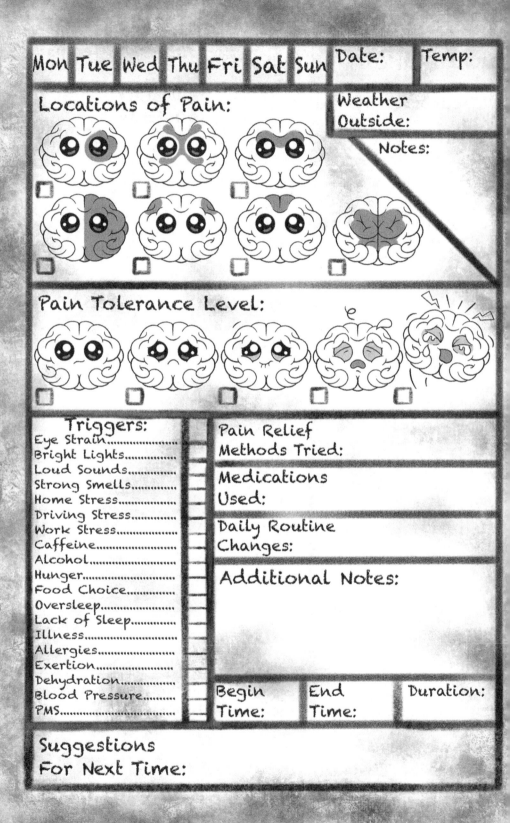

Mon | Tue | Wed | Thu | Fri | Sat | Sun | Date: | Temp:

Locations of Pain:

Weather Outside:

Notes:

Pain Tolerance Level:

Triggers:
Eye Strain...............
Bright Lights...............
Loud Sounds...............
Strong Smells...............
Home Stress...............
Driving Stress...............
Work Stress...............
Caffeine...............
Alcohol...............
Hunger...............
Food Choice...............
Oversleep...............
Lack of Sleep...............
Illness...............
Allergies...............
Exertion...............
Dehydration...............
Blood Pressure...........
PMS...............

Pain Relief Methods Tried:

Medications Used:

Daily Routine Changes:

Additional Notes:

Begin Time: | End Time: | Duration:

Suggestions For Next Time:

Mon | Tue | Wed | Thu | Fri | Sat | Sun | Date: | Temp:

Locations of Pain:

Weather Outside:

Notes:

Pain Tolerance Level:

Triggers:

Eye Strain..............
Bright Lights..............
Loud Sounds..............
Strong Smells..............
Home Stress..............
Driving Stress..............
Work Stress..............
Caffeine..............
Alcohol..............
Hunger..............
Food Choice..............
Oversleep..............
Lack of Sleep..............
Illness..............
Allergies..............
Exertion..............
Dehydration..............
Blood Pressure..........
PMS..............

Pain Relief Methods Tried:

Medications Used:

Daily Routine Changes:

Additional Notes:

Begin Time: | End Time: | Duration:

Suggestions For Next Time:

Mon	Tue	Wed	Thu	Fri	Sat	Sun	Date:	Temp:

Locations of Pain:

Weather
Outside:

Notes:

Pain Tolerance Level:

Triggers:

Eye Strain.................
Bright Lights.............
Loud Sounds..............
Strong Smells............
Home Stress..............
Driving Stress...........
Work Stress..............
Caffeine....................
Alcohol.....................
Hunger......................
Food Choice..............
Oversleep..................
Lack of Sleep............
Illness......................
Allergies...................
Exertion...................
Dehydration..............
Blood Pressure..........
PMS..........................

Pain Relief
Methods Tried:

Medications
Used:

Daily Routine
Changes:

Additional Notes:

Begin Time:	End Time:	Duration:

Suggestions
For Next Time:

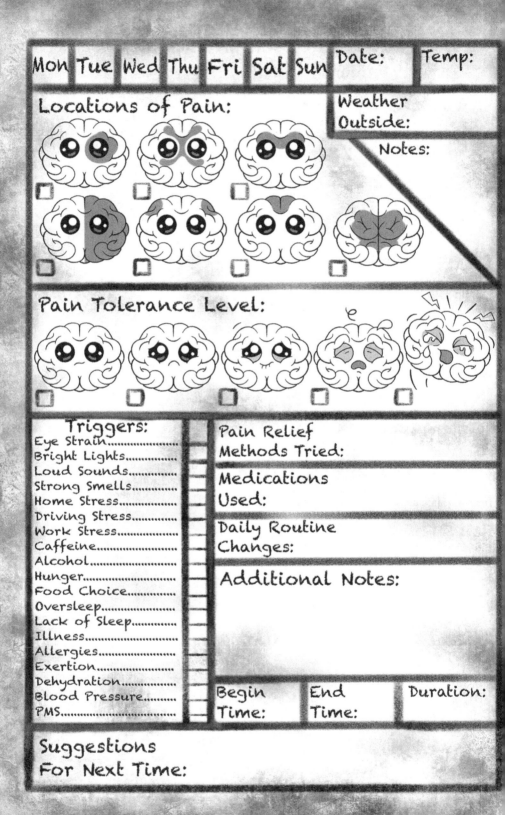

| Mon | Tue | Wed | Thu | Fri | Sat | Sun | Date: | Temp: |

Locations of Pain:

Weather Outside:

Notes:

Pain Tolerance Level:

Triggers:

Eye Strain................
Bright Lights...............
Loud Sounds..............
Strong Smells.............
Home Stress...............
Driving Stress.............
Work Stress................
Caffeine.....................
Alcohol.......................
Hunger.......................
Food Choice...............
Oversleep...................
Lack of Sleep.............
Illness........................
Allergies.....................
Exertion.....................
Dehydration...............
Blood Pressure...........
PMS...........................

Pain Relief Methods Tried:

Medications Used:

Daily Routine Changes:

Additional Notes:

Begin Time:

End Time:

Duration:

Suggestions For Next Time:

| Mon | Tue | Wed | Thu | Fri | Sat | Sun | Date: | Temp: |

Locations of Pain:

Weather
Outside:

Notes:

Pain Tolerance Level:

Triggers:
Eye Strain...................
Bright Lights...............
Loud Sounds...............
Strong Smells.............
Home Stress...............
Driving Stress.............
Work Stress.................
Caffeine......................
Alcohol........................
Hunger........................
Food Choice...............
Oversleep....................
Lack of Sleep..............
Illness.........................
Allergies......................
Exertion......................
Dehydration................
Blood Pressure............
PMS..............................

Pain Relief
Methods Tried:

Medications
Used:

Daily Routine
Changes:

Additional Notes:

Begin
Time:

End
Time:

Duration:

Suggestions
For Next Time:

| Mon | Tue | Wed | Thu | Fri | Sat | Sun | Date: | Temp: |

Locations of Pain:

Weather Outside:

Notes:

Pain Tolerance Level:

Triggers:

Eye Strain............
Bright Lights..............
Loud Sounds.............
Strong Smells..........
Home Stress............
Driving Stress..........
Work Stress.............
Caffeine.................
Alcohol...................
Hunger....................
Food Choice.............
Oversleep................
Lack of Sleep...........
Illness...................
Allergies.................
Exertion..................
Dehydration.............
Blood Pressure..........
PMS.......................

Pain Relief Methods Tried:

Medications Used:

Daily Routine Changes:

Additional Notes:

Begin Time:

End Time:

Duration:

Suggestions For Next Time:

| Mon | Tue | Wed | Thu | Fri | Sat | Sun | Date: | Temp: |

Locations of Pain:

Weather Outside:

Notes:

Pain Tolerance Level:

Triggers:
Eye Strain..................
Bright Lights................
Loud Sounds...............
Strong Smells..............
Home Stress...............
Driving Stress.............
Work Stress................
Caffeine......................
Alcohol.......................
Hunger.......................
Food Choice...............
Oversleep....................
Lack of Sleep.............
Illness........................
Allergies.....................
Exertion.....................
Dehydration...............
Blood Pressure...........
PMS...........................

Pain Relief Methods Tried:

Medications Used:

Daily Routine Changes:

Additional Notes:

Begin Time:

End Time:

Duration:

Suggestions For Next Time:

| Mon | Tue | Wed | Thu | Fri | Sat | Sun | Date: | Temp: |

Locations of Pain:

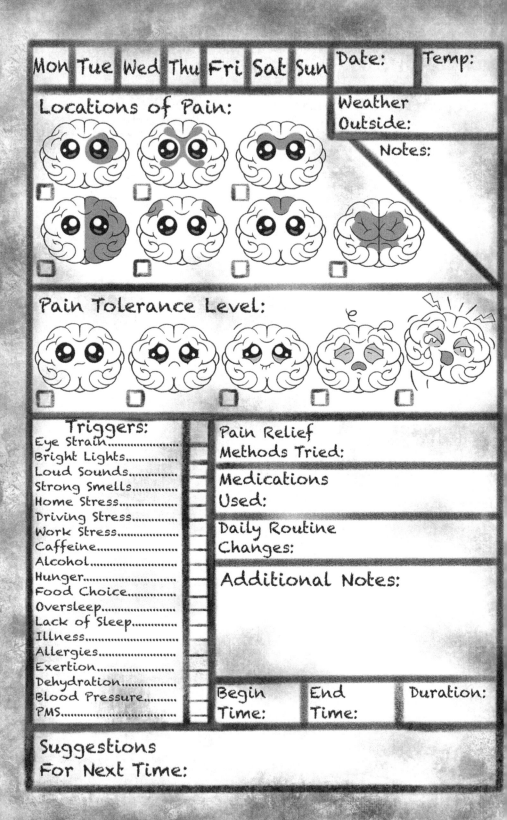

Weather
Outside:

Notes:

☐   ☐   ☐

☐   ☐   ☐   ☐

Pain Tolerance Level:

☐   ☐   ☐   ☐   ☐

Triggers:
Eye Strain.................
Bright Lights...............
Loud Sounds................
Strong Smells...............
Home Stress................
Driving Stress.............
Work Stress.................
Caffeine.......................
Alcohol.........................
Hunger..........................
Food Choice...............
Oversleep.....................
Lack of Sleep.............
Illness...........................
Allergies.......................
Exertion.......................
Dehydration................
Blood Pressure..........
PMS................................

Pain Relief
Methods Tried:

Medications
Used:

Daily Routine
Changes:

Additional Notes:

| Begin Time: | End Time: | Duration: |

Suggestions For Next Time:

| Mon | Tue | Wed | Thu | Fri | Sat | Sun | Date: | Temp: |

Locations of Pain:

Weather
Outside:

Notes:

Pain Tolerance Level:

Triggers:

Eye Strain.....................
Bright Lights................
Loud Sounds.................
Strong Smells...............
Home Stress..................
Driving Stress...............
Work Stress...................
Caffeine.........................
Alcohol...........................
Hunger............................
Food Choice.................
Oversleep.......................
Lack of Sleep...............
Illness.............................
Allergies.........................
Exertion..........................
Dehydration...................
Blood Pressure.............
PMS.................................

Pain Relief
Methods Tried:

Medications
Used:

Daily Routine
Changes:

Additional Notes:

Begin
Time:

End
Time:

Duration:

**Suggestions
For Next Time:**

| Mon | Tue | Wed | Thu | Fri | Sat | Sun | Date: | Temp: |

Locations of Pain:

Weather
Outside:

Notes:

Pain Tolerance Level:

Triggers:
Eye Strain...................
Bright Lights...............
Loud Sounds................
Strong Smells..............
Home Stress................
Driving Stress..............
Work Stress.................
Caffeine......................
Alcohol.......................
Hunger........................
Food Choice................
Oversleep.....................
Lack of Sleep..............
Illness.........................
Allergies......................
Exertion......................
Dehydration................
Blood Pressure...........
PMS............................

Pain Relief
Methods Tried:

Medications
Used:

Daily Routine
Changes:

Additional Notes:

Begin
Time:

End
Time:

Duration:

Suggestions
For Next Time:

| Mon | Tue | Wed | Thu | Fri | Sat | Sun | Date: | Temp: |

Locations of Pain:

Weather
Outside:

Notes:

☐   ☐   ☐

☐   ☐   ☐   ☐

Pain Tolerance Level:

☐   ☐   ☐   ☐   ☐

Triggers:

Eye Strain..................
Bright Lights..............
Loud Sounds..............
Strong Smells.............
Home Stress...............
Driving Stress.............
Work Stress................
Caffeine.....................
Alcohol......................
Hunger......................
Food Choice...............
Oversleep...................
Lack of Sleep..............
Illness........................
Allergies.....................
Exertion.....................
Dehydration...............
Blood Pressure...........
PMS..........................

**Pain Relief
Methods Tried:**

**Medications
Used:**

**Daily Routine
Changes:**

Additional Notes:

Begin
Time:

End
Time:

Duration:

**Suggestions
For Next Time:**

| Mon | Tue | Wed | Thu | Fri | Sat | Sun | Date: | Temp: |

Locations of Pain:

Weather Outside:

Notes:

Pain Tolerance Level:

Triggers:

Eye Strain.................
Bright Lights..............
Loud Sounds..............
Strong Smells............
Home Stress..............
Driving Stress............
Work Stress...............
Caffeine....................
Alcohol.....................
Hunger......................
Food Choice..............
Oversleep..................
Lack of Sleep.............
Illness......................
Allergies....................
Exertion.....................
Dehydration...............
Blood Pressure...........
PMS..........................

Pain Relief Methods Tried:

Medications Used:

Daily Routine Changes:

Additional Notes:

Begin Time:

End Time:

Duration:

Suggestions For Next Time:

Mon	Tue	Wed	Thu	Fri	Sat	Sun	Date:	Temp:

Locations of Pain:

Weather
Outside:

Notes:

Pain Tolerance Level:

Triggers:
Eye Strain......................
Bright Lights.................
Loud Sounds................
Strong Smells................
Home Stress..................
Driving Stress..............
Work Stress...................
Caffeine.........................
Alcohol...........................
Hunger...........................
Food Choice..................
Oversleep.......................
Lack of Sleep...............
Illness............................
Allergies........................
Exertion.........................
Dehydration..................
Blood Pressure...........
PMS.................................

Pain Relief
Methods Tried:

Medications
Used:

Daily Routine
Changes:

Additional Notes:

Begin Time:	End Time:	Duration:

Suggestions
For Next Time:

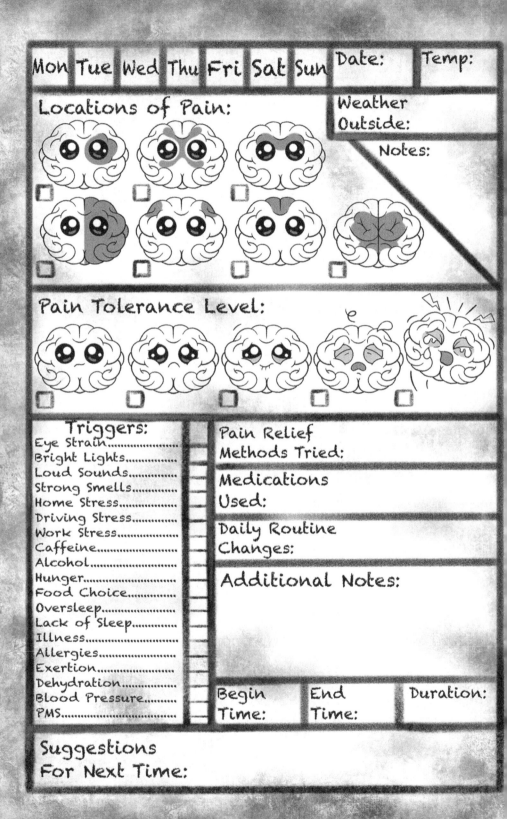

Mon | Tue | Wed | Thu | Fri | Sat | Sun

Date:

Temp:

Locations of Pain:

Weather Outside:

Notes:

Pain Tolerance Level:

Triggers:
Eye Strain.......................
Bright Lights................
Loud Sounds................
Strong Smells..............
Home Stress.................
Driving Stress..............
Work Stress..................
Caffeine........................
Alcohol.........................
Hunger..........................
Food Choice.................
Oversleep......................
Lack of Sleep...............
Illness............................
Allergies.......................
Exertion........................
Dehydration..................
Blood Pressure...........
PMS................................

Pain Relief Methods Tried:

Medications Used:

Daily Routine Changes:

Additional Notes:

Begin Time:

End Time:

Duration:

Suggestions For Next Time:

| Mon | Tue | Wed | Thu | Fri | Sat | Sun | Date: | Temp: |

Locations of Pain:

Weather
Outside:

Notes:

Pain Tolerance Level:

Triggers:

Eye Strain...............
Bright Lights...........
Loud Sounds...........
Strong Smells.........
Home Stress...........
Driving Stress.........
Work Stress...........
Caffeine...............
Alcohol................
Hunger................
Food Choice..........
Oversleep.............
Lack of Sleep.........
Illness................
Allergies..............
Exertion..............
Dehydration..........
Blood Pressure.......
PMS...................

Pain Relief
Methods Tried:

Medications
Used:

Daily Routine
Changes:

Additional Notes:

| Begin Time: | End Time: | Duration: |

Suggestions For Next Time:

Mon	Tue	Wed	Thu	Fri	Sat	Sun	Date:	Temp:

Locations of Pain:

Weather
Outside:

Notes:

Pain Tolerance Level:

Triggers:

Eye Strain..................
Bright Lights...............
Loud Sounds...............
Strong Smells.............
Home Stress...............
Driving Stress.............
Work Stress................
Caffeine.....................
Alcohol......................
Hunger.......................
Food Choice...............
Oversleep...................
Lack of Sleep.............
Illness........................
Allergies.....................
Exertion.....................
Dehydration...............
Blood Pressure..........
PMS...........................

Pain Relief
Methods Tried:

Medications
Used:

Daily Routine
Changes:

Additional Notes:

Begin Time:	End Time:	Duration:

Suggestions
For Next Time:

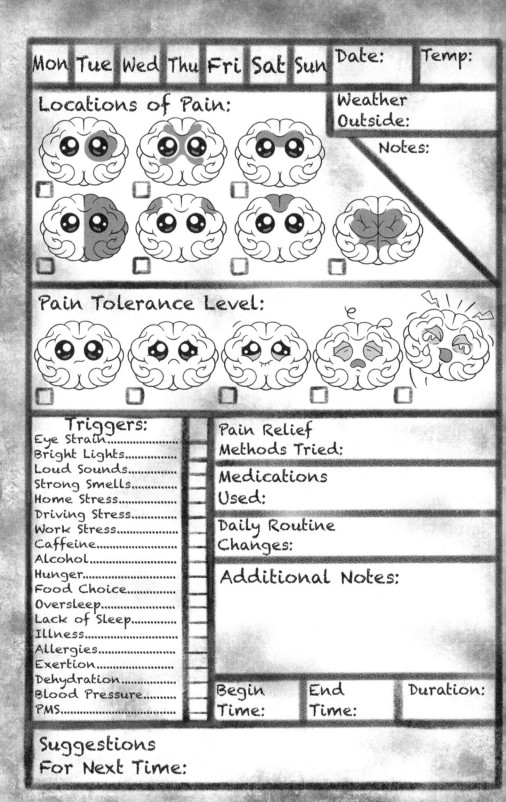

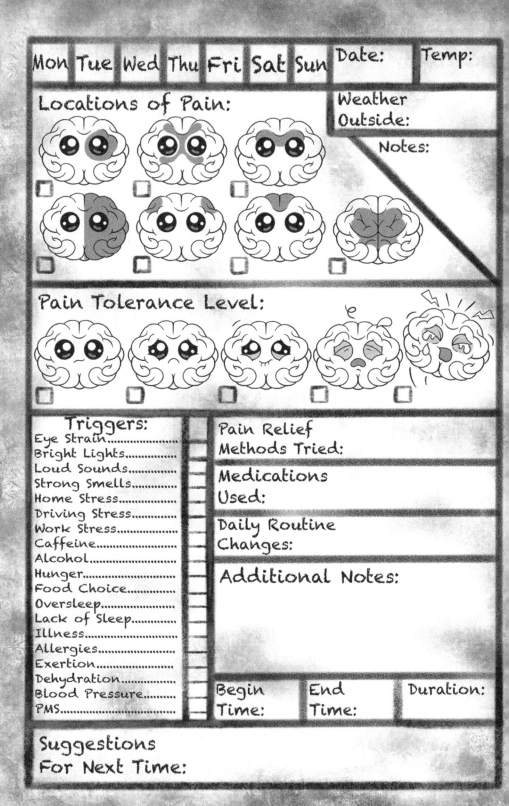

| Mon | Tue | Wed | Thu | Fri | Sat | Sun | Date: | Temp: |

Locations of Pain:

Weather Outside:

Notes:

Pain Tolerance Level:

Triggers:
Eye Strain..........................
Bright Lights.....................
Loud Sounds.....................
Strong Smells...................
Home Stress.......................
Driving Stress..................
Work Stress........................
Caffeine.............................
Alcohol..............................
Hunger..............................
Food Choice....................
Oversleep.........................
Lack of Sleep.................
Illness...............................
Allergies...........................
Exertion............................
Dehydration...................
Blood Pressure...........
PMS....................................

Pain Relief Methods Tried:

Medications Used:

Daily Routine Changes:

Additional Notes:

Begin Time:

End Time:

Duration:

Suggestions For Next Time:

Mon Tue Wed Thu Fri Sat Sun   Date: Temp:

Locations of Pain:

Weather Outside:

Notes:

Pain Tolerance Level:

Triggers:
Eye Strain...............
Bright Lights..............
Loud Sounds...............
Strong Smells............
Home Stress................
Driving Stress.............
Work Stress.................
Caffeine......................
Alcohol.......................
Hunger........................
Food Choice...............
Oversleep....................
Lack of Sleep.............
Illness.........................
Allergies.....................
Exertion......................
Dehydration...............
Blood Pressure..........
PMS............................

Pain Relief Methods Tried:

Medications Used:

Daily Routine Changes:

Additional Notes:

Begin Time: End Time: Duration:

Suggestions For Next Time:

| Mon | Tue | Wed | Thu | Fri | Sat | Sun | Date: | Temp: |

Locations of Pain:

Weather Outside:

Notes:

Pain Tolerance Level:

Triggers:

Eye Strain............
Bright Lights.................
Loud Sounds................
Strong Smells...............
Home Stress..................
Driving Stress..............
Work Stress..................
Caffeine.......................
Alcohol.........................
Hunger...........................
Food Choice...............
Oversleep.......................
Lack of Sleep.............
Illness............................
Allergies.......................
Exertion........................
Dehydration.................
Blood Pressure...........
PMS................................

Pain Relief Methods Tried:

Medications Used:

Daily Routine Changes:

Additional Notes:

| Begin Time: | End Time: | Duration: |

Suggestions For Next Time:

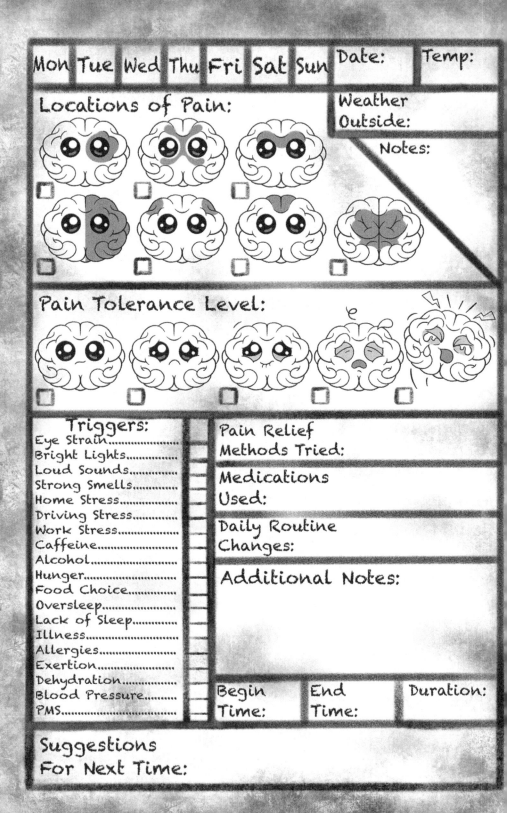

| Mon | Tue | Wed | Thu | Fri | Sat | Sun | Date: | Temp: |

Locations of Pain:

Weather
Outside:

Notes:

☐ ☐ ☐

☐ ☐ ☐ ☐

Pain Tolerance Level:

☐ ☐ ☐ ☐ ☐

Triggers:

Eye Strain...............
Bright Lights...............
Loud Sounds...............
Strong Smells...............
Home Stress...............
Driving Stress...............
Work Stress...............
Caffeine...............
Alcohol...............
Hunger...............
Food Choice...............
Oversleep...............
Lack of Sleep...............
Illness...............
Allergies...............
Exertion...............
Dehydration...............
Blood Pressure...............
PMS...............

Pain Relief
Methods Tried:

Medications
Used:

Daily Routine
Changes:

Additional Notes:

| Begin Time: | End Time: | Duration: |

Suggestions For Next Time:

Mon Tue Wed Thu Fri Sat Sun Date: Temp:

Locations of Pain:

Weather Outside:

Notes:

Pain Tolerance Level:

Triggers:
Eye Strain...............
Bright Lights...............
Loud Sounds...............
Strong Smells...............
Home Stress...............
Driving Stress...............
Work Stress...............
Caffeine...............
Alcohol...............
Hunger...............
Food Choice...............
Oversleep...............
Lack of Sleep...............
Illness...............
Allergies...............
Exertion...............
Dehydration...............
Blood Pressure...........
PMS...............

Pain Relief Methods Tried:

Medications Used:

Daily Routine Changes:

Additional Notes:

Begin Time:

End Time:

Duration:

Suggestions For Next Time:

| Mon | Tue | Wed | Thu | Fri | Sat | Sun | Date: | Temp: |

Locations of Pain:

Weather
Outside:

Notes:

Pain Tolerance Level:

Triggers:

Eye Strain..................
Bright Lights..............
Loud Sounds..............
Strong Smells............
Home Stress..............
Driving Stress............
Work Stress...............
Caffeine....................
Alcohol......................
Hunger......................
Food Choice..............
Oversleep..................
Lack of Sleep............
Illness.......................
Allergies....................
Exertion.....................
Dehydration..............
Blood Pressure..........
PMS...........................

Pain Relief
Methods Tried:

Medications
Used:

Daily Routine
Changes:

Additional Notes:

Begin
Time:

End
Time:

Duration:

Suggestions
For Next Time:

Mon Tue Wed Thu Fri Sat Sun Date: Temp:

Locations of Pain:

Weather Outside:

Notes:

Pain Tolerance Level:

Triggers:
Eye Strain.......................
Bright Lights................
Loud Sounds................
Strong Smells..............
Home Stress..................
Driving Stress..............
Work Stress..................
Caffeine...........................
Alcohol.............................
Hunger.............................
Food Choice...............
Oversleep......................
Lack of Sleep..............
Illness.............................
Allergies.........................
Exertion.........................
Dehydration................
Blood Pressure.........
PMS...................................

Pain Relief
Methods Tried:

Medications
Used:

Daily Routine
Changes:

Additional Notes:

Begin
Time:

End
Time:

Duration:

Suggestions
For Next Time:

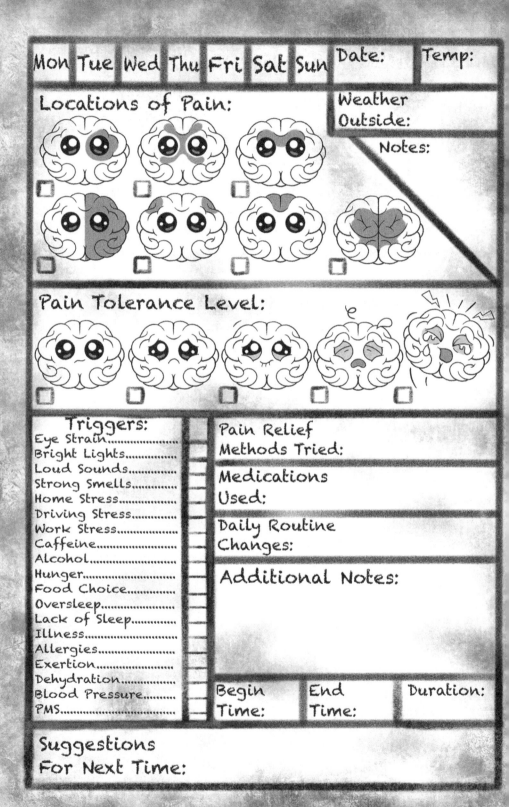

| Mon | Tue | Wed | Thu | Fri | Sat | Sun | Date: | Temp: |

Locations of Pain:

Weather Outside:

Notes:

Pain Tolerance Level:

Triggers:

Eye Strain...............
Bright Lights...............
Loud Sounds...............
Strong Smells...............
Home Stress...............
Driving Stress...............
Work Stress...............
Caffeine...............
Alcohol...............
Hunger...............
Food Choice...............
Oversleep...............
Lack of Sleep...............
Illness...............
Allergies...............
Exertion...............
Dehydration...............
Blood Pressure...........
PMS...............

Pain Relief Methods Tried:

Medications Used:

Daily Routine Changes:

Additional Notes:

Begin Time:

End Time:

Duration:

Suggestions For Next Time:

Mon	Tue	Wed	Thu	Fri	Sat	Sun	Date:	Temp:

Locations of Pain:

Weather
Outside:

Notes:

Pain Tolerance Level:

Triggers:

Eye Strain..................
Bright Lights..............
Loud Sounds..............
Strong Smells............
Home Stress..............
Driving Stress............
Work Stress...............
Caffeine....................
Alcohol.....................
Hunger......................
Food Choice..............
Oversleep..................
Lack of Sleep............
Illness......................
Allergies...................
Exertion....................
Dehydration..............
Blood Pressure..........
PMS.........................

Pain Relief
Methods Tried:

Medications
Used:

Daily Routine
Changes:

Additional Notes:

Begin Time:	End Time:	Duration:

Suggestions
For Next Time:

Mon | Tue | Wed | Thu | Fri | Sat | Sun | Date: | Temp:

Locations of Pain:

Weather Outside:

Notes:

Pain Tolerance Level:

Triggers:
Eye Strain...............
Bright Lights.............
Loud Sounds.............
Strong Smells...........
Home Stress..............
Driving Stress...........
Work Stress..............
Caffeine..................
Alcohol....................
Hunger....................
Food Choice.............
Oversleep.................
Lack of Sleep............
Illness.....................
Allergies..................
Exertion...................
Dehydration.............
Blood Pressure..........
PMS........................

Pain Relief
Methods Tried:

Medications
Used:

Daily Routine
Changes:

Additional Notes:

Begin Time: | End Time: | Duration:

Suggestions For Next Time:

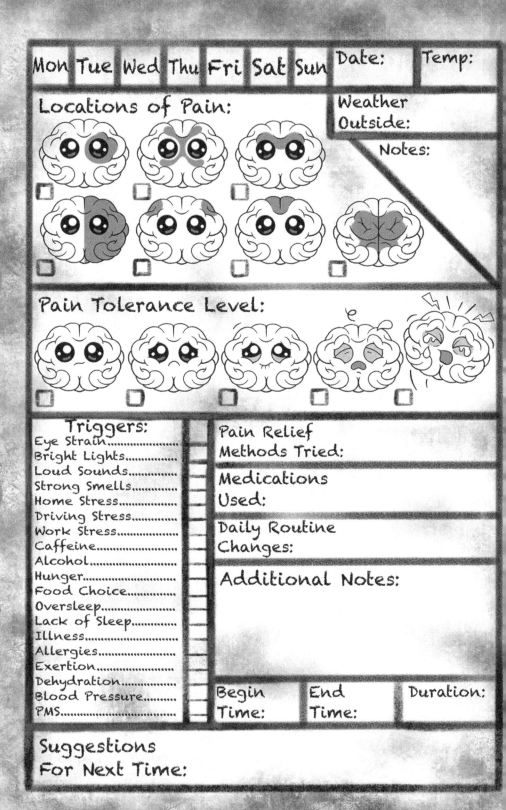

| Mon | Tue | Wed | Thu | Fri | Sat | Sun | Date: | Temp: |

Locations of Pain:

Weather Outside:

Notes:

Pain Tolerance Level:

Triggers:

Eye Strain..........................
Bright Lights.....................
Loud Sounds......................
Strong Smells....................
Home Stress.......................
Driving Stress....................
Work Stress.......................
Caffeine.............................
Alcohol..............................
Hunger..............................
Food Choice......................
Oversleep..........................
Lack of Sleep...................
Illness..............................
Allergies...........................
Exertion............................
Dehydration......................
Blood Pressure..............
PMS...................................

Pain Relief Methods Tried:

Medications Used:

Daily Routine Changes:

Additional Notes:

Begin Time:

End Time:

Duration:

Suggestions For Next Time:

Mon	Tue	Wed	Thu	Fri	Sat	Sun	Date:	Temp:

Locations of Pain:

Weather Outside:

Notes:

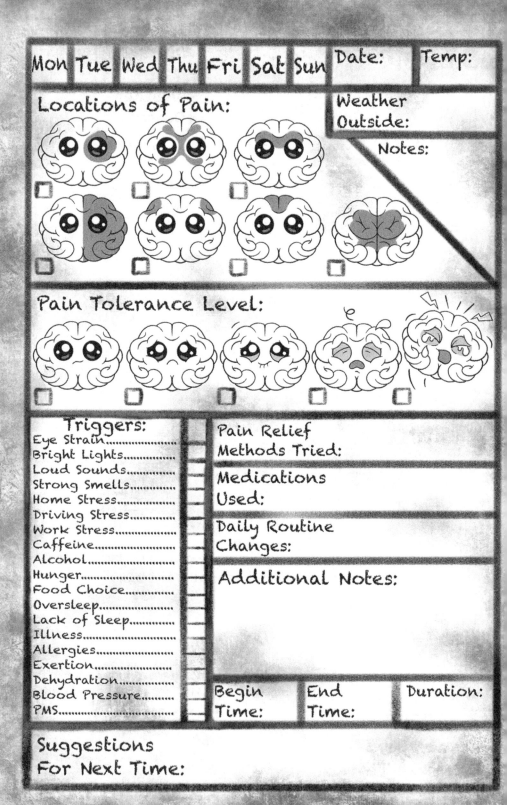

Pain Tolerance Level:

Triggers:

Eye Strain...................
Bright Lights................
Loud Sounds................
Strong Smells..............
Home Stress................
Driving Stress.............
Work Stress................
Caffeine.....................
Alcohol......................
Hunger......................
Food Choice...............
Oversleep...................
Lack of Sleep..............
Illness.......................
Allergies....................
Exertion....................
Dehydration...............
Blood Pressure..........
PMS..........................

Pain Relief Methods Tried:

Medications Used:

Daily Routine Changes:

Additional Notes:

Begin Time:	End Time:	Duration:

Suggestions For Next Time:

| Mon | Tue | Wed | Thu | Fri | Sat | Sun | Date: | Temp: |

Locations of Pain:

Weather
Outside:

Notes:

Pain Tolerance Level:

Triggers:
Eye Strain..................
Bright Lights..............
Loud Sounds..............
Strong Smells.............
Home Stress...............
Driving Stress............
Work Stress................
Caffeine......................
Alcohol.......................
Hunger.......................
Food Choice...............
Oversleep...................
Lack of Sleep.............
Illness........................
Allergies.....................
Exertion......................
Dehydration...............
Blood Pressure..........
PMS...........................

Pain Relief
Methods Tried:

Medications
Used:

Daily Routine
Changes:

Additional Notes:

Begin
Time:

End
Time:

Duration:

Suggestions
For Next Time:

| Mon | Tue | Wed | Thu | Fri | Sat | Sun | Date: | Temp: |

Locations of Pain:

Weather Outside:

Notes:

Pain Tolerance Level:

Triggers:

Eye Strain.................
Bright Lights................
Loud Sounds...............
Strong Smells..............
Home Stress.................
Driving Stress.............
Work Stress..................
Caffeine.......................
Alcohol.........................
Hunger.........................
Food Choice.................
Oversleep.....................
Lack of Sleep..............
Illness...........................
Allergies.......................
Exertion........................
Dehydration.................
Blood Pressure..........
PMS...............................

Pain Relief Methods Tried:

Medications Used:

Daily Routine Changes:

Additional Notes:

Begin Time:

End Time:

Duration:

Suggestions For Next Time:

| Mon | Tue | Wed | Thu | Fri | Sat | Sun | Date: | Temp: |

Locations of Pain:

Weather Outside:

Notes:

Pain Tolerance Level:

Triggers:

Eye Strain....................
Bright Lights................
Loud Sounds................
Strong Smells..............
Home Stress................
Driving Stress.............
Work Stress................
Caffeine........................
Alcohol.........................
Hunger.........................
Food Choice................
Oversleep.....................
Lack of Sleep..............
Illness..........................
Allergies......................
Exertion.......................
Dehydration................
Blood Pressure...........
PMS..............................

Pain Relief Methods Tried:

Medications Used:

Daily Routine Changes:

Additional Notes:

| Begin Time: | End Time: | Duration: |

Suggestions For Next Time:

| Mon | Tue | Wed | Thu | Fri | Sat | Sun | Date: | Temp: |

Locations of Pain:

Weather Outside:

Notes:

Pain Tolerance Level:

Triggers:

Eye Strain.........................
Bright Lights....................
Loud Sounds....................
Strong Smells..................
Home Stress.....................
Driving Stress.................
Work Stress......................
Caffeine............................
Alcohol..............................
Hunger...............................
Food Choice.....................
Oversleep..........................
Lack of Sleep..................
Illness................................
Allergies............................
Exertion............................
Dehydration......................
Blood Pressure..............
PMS....................................

Pain Relief Methods Tried:

Medications Used:

Daily Routine Changes:

Additional Notes:

Begin Time:

End Time:

Duration:

Suggestions For Next Time:

Mon | Tue | Wed | Thu | Fri | Sat | Sun   Date: Temp:

Locations of Pain:

Weather
Outside:

Notes:

Pain Tolerance Level:

Triggers:
Eye Strain................
Bright Lights...............
Loud Sounds..............
Strong Smells.............
Home Stress..............
Driving Stress.............
Work Stress................
Caffeine....................
Alcohol.....................
Hunger.....................
Food Choice...............
Oversleep..................
Lack of Sleep.............
Illness......................
Allergies....................
Exertion....................
Dehydration...............
Blood Pressure..........
PMS.........................

Pain Relief
Methods Tried:

Medications
Used:

Daily Routine
Changes:

Additional Notes:

Begin
Time:

End
Time:

Duration:

Suggestions
For Next Time:

Mon	Tue	Wed	Thu	Fri	Sat	Sun	Date:	Temp:

Locations of Pain:

Weather Outside:

Notes:

Pain Tolerance Level:

Triggers:
Eye Strain............
Bright Lights............
Loud Sounds............
Strong Smells............
Home Stress............
Driving Stress............
Work Stress............
Caffeine............
Alcohol............
Hunger............
Food Choice............
Oversleep............
Lack of Sleep............
Illness............
Allergies............
Exertion............
Dehydration............
Blood Pressure............
PMS............

Pain Relief Methods Tried:

Medications Used:

Daily Routine Changes:

Additional Notes:

Begin Time:	End Time:	Duration:

Suggestions For Next Time:

| Mon | Tue | Wed | Thu | Fri | Sat | Sun | Date: | Temp: |

Locations of Pain:

Weather
Outside:

Notes:

Pain Tolerance Level:

Triggers:
Eye Strain...............
Bright Lights...........
Loud Sounds............
Strong Smells..........
Home Stress............
Driving Stress..........
Work Stress.............
Caffeine..................
Alcohol...................
Hunger...................
Food Choice............
Oversleep................
Lack of Sleep...........
Illness....................
Allergies.................
Exertion.................
Dehydration............
Blood Pressure.........
PMS.......................

Pain Relief
Methods Tried:

Medications
Used:

Daily Routine
Changes:

Additional Notes:

Begin
Time:

End
Time:

Duration:

Suggestions
For Next Time:

| Mon | Tue | Wed | Thu | Fri | Sat | Sun | Date: | Temp: |

Locations of Pain:

Weather Outside:

Notes:

Pain Tolerance Level:

Triggers:
Eye Strain...................
Bright Lights...............
Loud Sounds...............
Strong Smells..............
Home Stress................
Driving Stress.............
Work Stress................
Caffeine......................
Alcohol.......................
Hunger.......................
Food Choice...............
Oversleep...................
Lack of Sleep.............
Illness........................
Allergies.....................
Exertion.....................
Dehydration...............
Blood Pressure..........
PMS...........................

Pain Relief Methods Tried:

Medications Used:

Daily Routine Changes:

Additional Notes:

Begin Time:

End Time:

Duration:

Suggestions For Next Time:

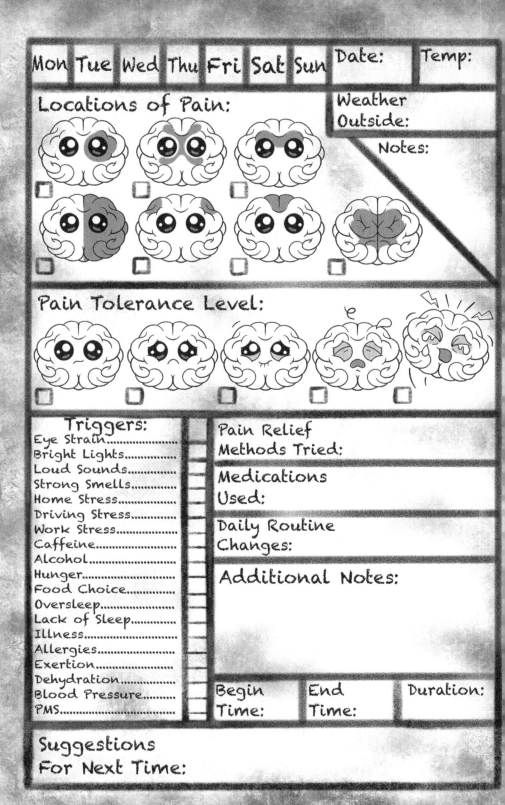

Mon	Tue	Wed	Thu	Fri	Sat	Sun	Date:	Temp:

Locations of Pain:

Weather
Outside:

Notes:

☐ ☐ ☐

☐ ☐ ☐ ☐

Pain Tolerance Level:

☐ ☐ ☐ ☐ ☐

Triggers:
Eye Strain.........................
Bright Lights...................
Loud Sounds..................
Strong Smells.................
Home Stress....................
Driving Stress................
Work Stress.....................
Caffeine............................
Alcohol..............................
Hunger..............................
Food Choice...................
Oversleep........................
Lack of Sleep.................
Illness...............................
Allergies...........................
Exertion............................
Dehydration..................
Blood Pressure...........
PMS...................................

Pain Relief
Methods Tried:

Medications
Used:

Daily Routine
Changes:

Additional Notes:

Begin Time:	End Time:	Duration:

Suggestions For Next Time:

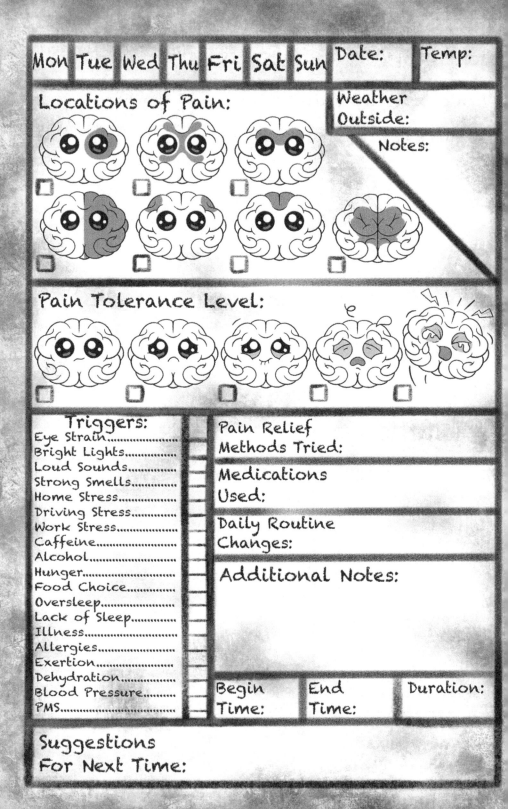

Mon Tue Wed Thu Fri Sat Sun

Date:

Temp:

Locations of Pain:

Weather Outside:

Notes:

Pain Tolerance Level:

Triggers:
Eye Strain......................
Bright Lights.................
Loud Sounds.................
Strong Smells...............
Home Stress.................
Driving Stress...............
Work Stress...................
Caffeine.........................
Alcohol..........................
Hunger...........................
Food Choice..................
Oversleep......................
Lack of Sleep...............
Illness............................
Allergies........................
Exertion.........................
Dehydration..................
Blood Pressure...........
PMS................................

Pain Relief Methods Tried:

Medications Used:

Daily Routine Changes:

Additional Notes:

Begin Time:

End Time:

Duration:

Suggestions For Next Time:

Mon	Tue	Wed	Thu	Fri	Sat	Sun	Date:	Temp:

Locations of Pain:

Weather
Outside:

Notes:

Pain Tolerance Level:

Triggers:
Eye Strain...............
Bright Lights.................
Loud Sounds................
Strong Smells...............
Home Stress..................
Driving Stress.............
Work Stress..................
Caffeine........................
Alcohol..........................
Hunger...........................
Food Choice...............
Oversleep.....................
Lack of Sleep.............
Illness...........................
Allergies.......................
Exertion.......................
Dehydration................
Blood Pressure..........
PMS..................................

Pain Relief
Methods Tried:

Medications
Used:

Daily Routine
Changes:

Additional Notes:

Begin
Time:

End
Time:

Duration:

Suggestions
For Next Time:

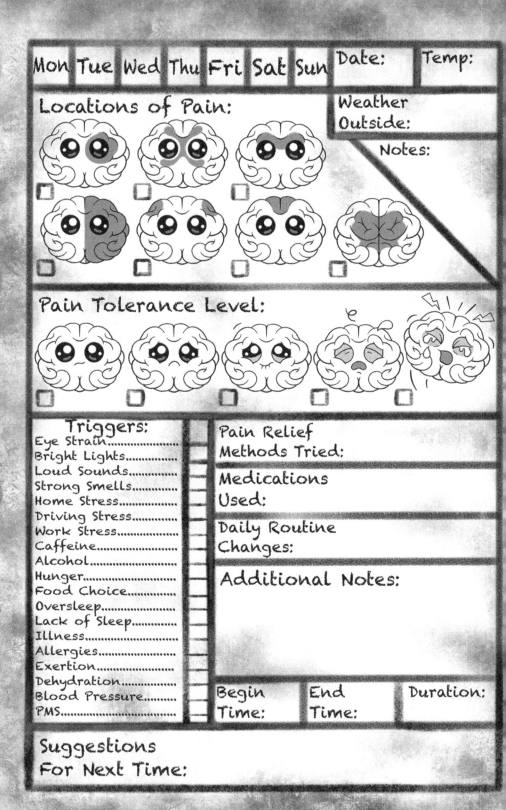

| Mon | Tue | Wed | Thu | Fri | Sat | Sun | Date: | Temp: |

Locations of Pain:

Weather
Outside:

Notes:

☐ ☐ ☐

☐ ☐ ☐ ☐

Pain Tolerance Level:

☐ ☐ ☐ ☐ ☐

Triggers:

Eye Strain...................
Bright Lights...............
Loud Sounds...............
Strong Smells..............
Home Stress................
Driving Stress..............
Work Stress.................
Caffeine.......................
Alcohol.........................
Hunger.........................
Food Choice.................
Oversleep.....................
Lack of Sleep...............
Illness..........................
Allergies.......................
Exertion.......................
Dehydration.................
Blood Pressure............
PMS..............................

**Pain Relief
Methods Tried:**

**Medications
Used:**

**Daily Routine
Changes:**

Additional Notes:

Begin
Time:

End
Time:

Duration:

**Suggestions
For Next Time:**

Mon	Tue	Wed	Thu	Fri	Sat	Sun	Date:	Temp:

Locations of Pain:

Weather
Outside:

Notes:

Pain Tolerance Level:

Triggers:

Eye Strain.......................
Bright Lights..................
Loud Sounds................
Strong Smells...............
Home Stress..................
Driving Stress...............
Work Stress...................
Caffeine.........................
Alcohol...........................
Hunger...........................
Food Choice..................
Oversleep......................
Lack of Sleep...............
Illness............................
Allergies.........................
Exertion.........................
Dehydration...................
Blood Pressure............
PMS.................................

Pain Relief
Methods Tried:

Medications
Used:

Daily Routine
Changes:

Additional Notes:

Begin
Time:

End
Time:

Duration:

Suggestions
For Next Time:

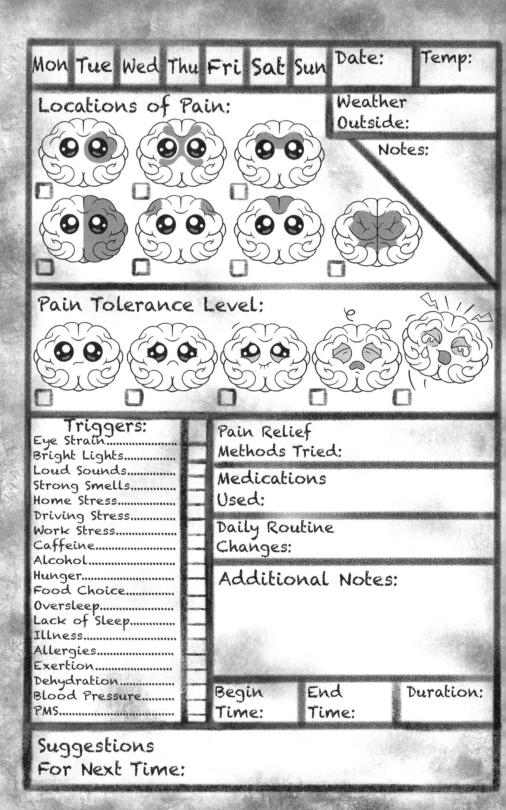

| Mon | Tue | Wed | Thu | Fri | Sat | Sun | Date: | Temp: |

Locations of Pain:

Weather
Outside:

Notes:

Pain Tolerance Level:

Triggers:

Eye Strain......................
Bright Lights..................
Loud Sounds..................
Strong Smells...............
Home Stress..................
Driving Stress...............
Work Stress..................
Caffeine..........................
Alcohol..........................
Hunger...........................
Food Choice..................
Oversleep......................
Lack of Sleep...............
Illness............................
Allergies........................
Exertion.........................
Dehydration..................
Blood Pressure...........
PMS.................................

Pain Relief
Methods Tried:

Medications
Used:

Daily Routine
Changes:

Additional Notes:

| Begin Time: | End Time: | Duration: |

Suggestions For Next Time:

| Mon | Tue | Wed | Thu | Fri | Sat | Sun | Date: | Temp: |

Locations of Pain:

Weather Outside:

Notes:

Pain Tolerance Level:

Triggers:
Eye Strain..................
Bright Lights.............
Loud Sounds.............
Strong Smells.............
Home Stress...............
Driving Stress.............
Work Stress...............
Caffeine.....................
Alcohol......................
Hunger......................
Food Choice..............
Oversleep...................
Lack of Sleep.............
Illness.......................
Allergies....................
Exertion.....................
Dehydration...............
Blood Pressure...........
PMS..........................

Pain Relief Methods Tried:

Medications Used:

Daily Routine Changes:

Additional Notes:

| Begin Time: | End Time: | Duration: |

Suggestions For Next Time:

| Mon | Tue | Wed | Thu | Fri | Sat | Sun | Date: | Temp: |

Locations of Pain:

Weather
Outside:

Notes:

Pain Tolerance Level:

Triggers:
Eye Strain.....................
Bright Lights................
Loud Sounds................
Strong Smells..............
Home Stress.................
Driving Stress..............
Work Stress..................
Caffeine.......................
Alcohol.........................
Hunger.........................
Food Choice................
Oversleep.....................
Lack of Sleep..............
Illness..........................
Allergies......................
Exertion.......................
Dehydration.................
Blood Pressure...........
PMS...............................

Pain Relief
Methods Tried:

Medications
Used:

Daily Routine
Changes:

Additional Notes:

Begin
Time:

End
Time:

Duration:

Suggestions
For Next Time:

| Mon | Tue | Wed | Thu | Fri | Sat | Sun | Date: | Temp: |

Locations of Pain:

Weather Outside:

Notes:

☐ ☐ ☐

☐ ☐ ☐

Pain Tolerance Level:

☐ ☐ ☐ ☐ ☐

Triggers:

Eye Strain..................
Bright Lights..............
Loud Sounds..............
Strong Smells............
Home Stress...............
Driving Stress............
Work Stress...............
Caffeine....................
Alcohol......................
Hunger......................
Food Choice..............
Oversleep...................
Lack of Sleep............
Illness.......................
Allergies...................
Exertion....................
Dehydration..............
Blood Pressure..........
PMS..........................

Pain Relief Methods Tried:

Medications Used:

Daily Routine Changes:

Additional Notes:

Begin Time:

End Time:

Duration:

Suggestions For Next Time:

Mon	Tue	Wed	Thu	Fri	Sat	Sun	Date:	Temp:

Locations of Pain:

Weather Outside:

Notes:

Pain Tolerance Level:

Triggers:

Eye Strain......................
Bright Lights.................
Loud Sounds.................
Strong Smells...............
Home Stress...................
Driving Stress...............
Work Stress...................
Caffeine..........................
Alcohol...........................
Hunger...........................
Food Choice.................
Oversleep......................
Lack of Sleep...............
Illness............................
Allergies........................
Exertion.........................
Dehydration.................
Blood Pressure...........
PMS................................

Pain Relief Methods Tried:

Medications Used:

Daily Routine Changes:

Additional Notes:

Begin Time:	End Time:	Duration:

Suggestions For Next Time:

| Mon | Tue | Wed | Thu | Fri | Sat | Sun | Date: | Temp: |

Locations of Pain:

Weather Outside:

Notes:

Pain Tolerance Level:

Triggers:

Eye Strain.....................
Bright Lights................
Loud Sounds................
Strong Smells..............
Home Stress.................
Driving Stress.............
Work Stress..................
Caffeine........................
Alcohol..........................
Hunger...........................
Food Choice................
Oversleep......................
Lack of Sleep..............
Illness............................
Allergies........................
Exertion.........................
Dehydration.................
Blood Pressure...........
PMS................................

Pain Relief
Methods Tried:

Medications
Used:

Daily Routine
Changes:

Additional Notes:

Begin
Time:

End
Time:

Duration:

Suggestions
For Next Time:

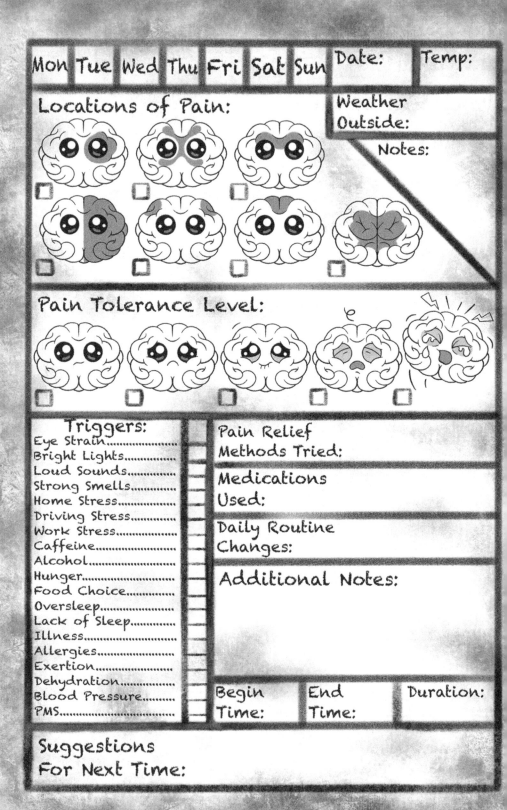

Mon Tue Wed Thu Fri Sat Sun | Date: | Temp:

Locations of Pain:

Weather Outside:

Notes:

Pain Tolerance Level:

Triggers:
Eye Strain.........................
Bright Lights.....................
Loud Sounds......................
Strong Smells....................
Home Stress......................
Driving Stress...................
Work Stress......................
Caffeine...........................
Alcohol............................
Hunger.............................
Food Choice......................
Oversleep.........................
Lack of Sleep....................
Illness.............................
Allergies..........................
Exertion...........................
Dehydration......................
Blood Pressure..................
PMS................................

Pain Relief
Methods Tried:

Medications
Used:

Daily Routine
Changes:

Additional Notes:

Begin Time: | End Time: | Duration:

Suggestions
For Next Time:

| Mon | Tue | Wed | Thu | Fri | Sat | Sun | Date: | Temp: |

Locations of Pain:

Weather Outside:

Notes:

Pain Tolerance Level:

Triggers:

Eye Strain...............
Bright Lights...............
Loud Sounds...............
Strong Smells...............
Home Stress...............
Driving Stress...............
Work Stress...............
Caffeine...............
Alcohol...............
Hunger...............
Food Choice...............
Oversleep...............
Lack of Sleep...............
Illness...............
Allergies...............
Exertion...............
Dehydration...............
Blood Pressure...............
PMS...............

Pain Relief Methods Tried:

Medications Used:

Daily Routine Changes:

Additional Notes:

Begin Time:

End Time:

Duration:

Suggestions For Next Time:

| Mon | Tue | Wed | Thu | Fri | Sat | Sun | Date: | Temp: |

Locations of Pain:

Weather
Outside:

Notes:

Pain Tolerance Level:

Triggers:
Eye Strain..............
Bright Lights................
Loud Sounds..............
Strong Smells..............
Home Stress..............
Driving Stress..............
Work Stress..............
Caffeine..............
Alcohol..............
Hunger..............
Food Choice..............
Oversleep..............
Lack of Sleep..............
Illness..............
Allergies..............
Exertion..............
Dehydration..............
Blood Pressure..........
PMS..............

Pain Relief
Methods Tried:

Medications
Used:

Daily Routine
Changes:

Additional Notes:

Begin
Time:

End
Time:

Duration:

Suggestions
For Next Time:

| Mon | Tue | Wed | Thu | Fri | Sat | Sun | Date: | Temp: |

Locations of Pain:

Weather Outside:

Notes:

Pain Tolerance Level:

Triggers:
Eye Strain..............
Bright Lights...............
Loud Sounds..............
Strong Smells..............
Home Stress...............
Driving Stress.............
Work Stress..............
Caffeine.................
Alcohol..................
Hunger...................
Food Choice..............
Oversleep................
Lack of Sleep............
Illness..................
Allergies................
Exertion.................
Dehydration...............
Blood Pressure..........
PMS.....................

Pain Relief
Methods Tried:

Medications
Used:

Daily Routine
Changes:

Additional Notes:

Begin
Time:

End
Time:

Duration:

Suggestions
For Next Time:

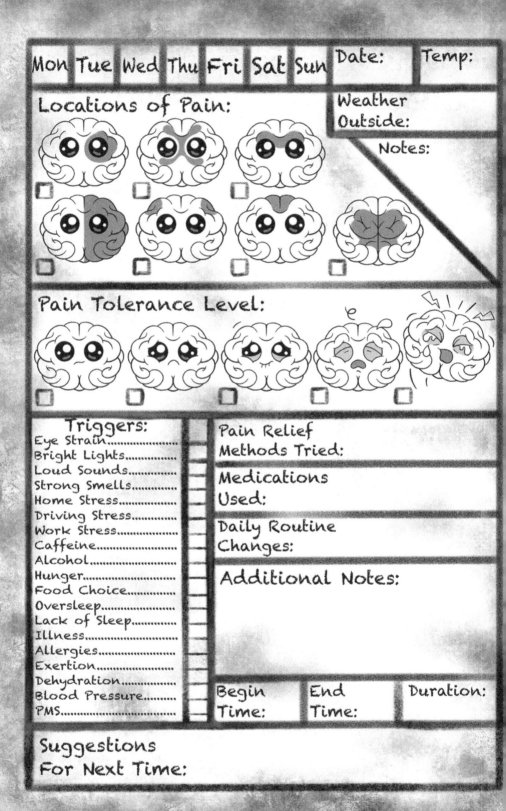

| Mon | Tue | Wed | Thu | Fri | Sat | Sun | Date: | Temp: |

Locations of Pain:

Weather Outside:

Notes:

☐ ☐ ☐

☐ ☐ ☐ ☐

Pain Tolerance Level:

☐ ☐ ☐ ☐ ☐

Triggers:

Eye Strain.................
Bright Lights.............
Loud Sounds..............
Strong Smells............
Home Stress..............
Driving Stress...........
Work Stress...............
Caffeine....................
Alcohol.....................
Hunger.....................
Food Choice..............
Oversleep..................
Lack of Sleep............
Illness.......................
Allergies...................
Exertion....................
Dehydration..............
Blood Pressure..........
PMS..........................

Pain Relief
Methods Tried:

Medications
Used:

Daily Routine
Changes:

Additional Notes:

| Begin Time: | End Time: | Duration: |

Suggestions
For Next Time:

Mon | Tue | Wed | Thu | Fri | Sat | Sun | Date: | Temp:

Locations of Pain:

Weather Outside:

Notes:

☐ ☐ ☐

☐ ☐ ☐ ☐

Pain Tolerance Level:

☐ ☐ ☐ ☐ ☐

Triggers:
Eye Strain...................
Bright Lights...............
Loud Sounds...............
Strong Smells.............
Home Stress...............
Driving Stress............
Work Stress................
Caffeine.......................
Alcohol.........................
Hunger.........................
Food Choice...............
Oversleep.....................
Lack of Sleep.............
Illness..........................
Allergies......................
Exertion.......................
Dehydration...............
Blood Pressure..........
PMS...............................

Pain Relief
Methods Tried:

Medications
Used:

Daily Routine
Changes:

Additional Notes:

Begin
Time: | End
Time: | Duration:

Suggestions
For Next Time:

Mon	Tue	Wed	Thu	Fri	Sat	Sun	Date:	Temp:

Locations of Pain:

Weather Outside:

Notes:

☐ ☐ ☐

☐ ☐ ☐ ☐

Pain Tolerance Level:

☐ ☐ ☐ ☐ ☐

Triggers:

Eye Strain..................
Bright Lights.............
Loud Sounds..............
Strong Smells.............
Home Stress...............
Driving Stress............
Work Stress...............
Caffeine.....................
Alcohol......................
Hunger.......................
Food Choice...............
Oversleep...................
Lack of Sleep.............
Illness.......................
Allergies....................
Exertion.....................
Dehydration...............
Blood Pressure..........
PMS...........................

Pain Relief Methods Tried:

Medications Used:

Daily Routine Changes:

Additional Notes:

Begin Time:	End Time:	Duration:

Suggestions For Next Time:

| Mon | Tue | Wed | Thu | Fri | Sat | Sun | Date: | Temp: |

Locations of Pain:

Weather Outside:

Notes:

Pain Tolerance Level:

Triggers:
Eye Strain.............
Bright Lights................
Loud Sounds...............
Strong Smells.............
Home Stress.................
Driving Stress.............
Work Stress.................
Caffeine......................
Alcohol......................
Hunger......................
Food Choice...............
Oversleep...................
Lack of Sleep...........
Illness......................
Allergies.................
Exertion...................
Dehydration..............
Blood Pressure...........
PMS..........................

Pain Relief Methods Tried:

Medications Used:

Daily Routine Changes:

Additional Notes:

Begin Time:

End Time:

Duration:

Suggestions For Next Time:

| Mon | Tue | Wed | Thu | Fri | Sat | Sun | Date: | Temp: |

Locations of Pain:

Weather
Outside:

Notes:

☐ ☐ ☐

☐ ☐ ☐

Pain Tolerance Level:

☐ ☐ ☐ ☐ ☐

Triggers:

Eye Strain.............
Bright Lights.............
Loud Sounds.............
Strong Smells.............
Home Stress.............
Driving Stress.............
Work Stress.............
Caffeine.............
Alcohol.............
Hunger.............
Food Choice.............
Oversleep.............
Lack of Sleep.............
Illness.............
Allergies.............
Exertion.............
Dehydration.............
Blood Pressure.............
PMS.............

Pain Relief
Methods Tried:

Medications
Used:

Daily Routine
Changes:

Additional Notes:

Begin
Time:

End
Time:

Duration:

Suggestions
For Next Time:

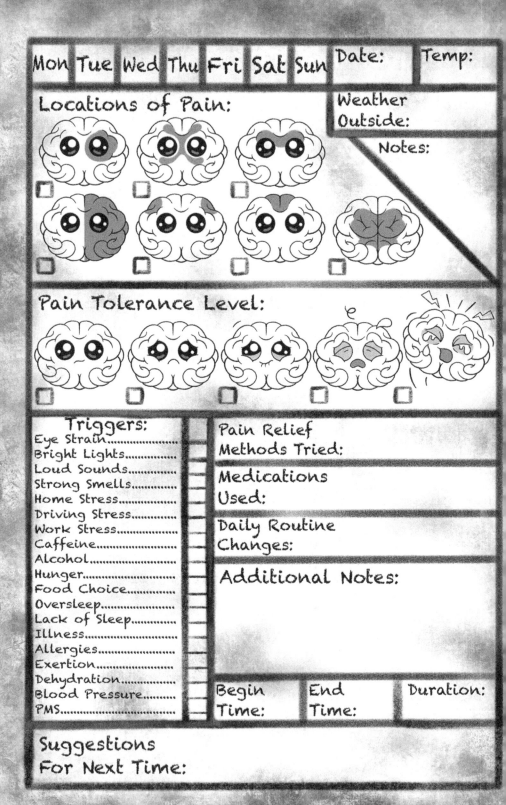

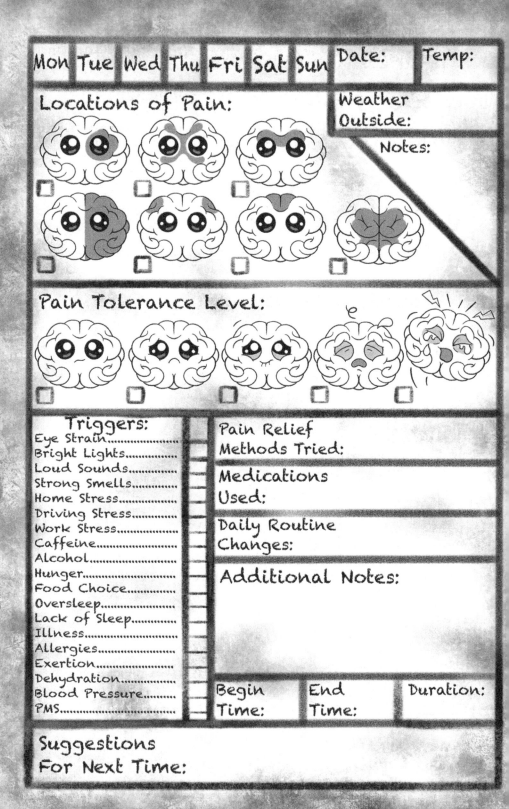

| Mon | Tue | Wed | Thu | Fri | Sat | Sun | Date: | Temp: |

Locations of Pain:

Weather Outside:

Notes:

Pain Tolerance Level:

Triggers:
Eye Strain...................
Bright Lights................
Loud Sounds................
Strong Smells..............
Home Stress................
Driving Stress.............
Work Stress.................
Caffeine......................
Alcohol.......................
Hunger........................
Food Choice...............
Oversleep....................
Lack of Sleep.............
Illness........................
Allergies.....................
Exertion.....................
Dehydration................
Blood Pressure..........
PMS............................

Pain Relief Methods Tried:

Medications Used:

Daily Routine Changes:

Additional Notes:

| Begin Time: | End Time: | Duration: |

Suggestions For Next Time:

| Mon | Tue | Wed | Thu | Fri | Sat | Sun | Date: | Temp: |

Locations of Pain:

Weather Outside:

Notes:

☐ ☐ ☐

☐ ☐ ☐ ☐

Pain Tolerance Level:

☐ ☐ ☐ ☐ ☐

Triggers:
Eye Strain.................
Bright Lights..............
Loud Sounds..............
Strong Smells.............
Home Stress..............
Driving Stress............
Work Stress...............
Caffeine....................
Alcohol.....................
Hunger......................
Food Choice...............
Oversleep..................
Lack of Sleep.............
Illness......................
Allergies....................
Exertion....................
Dehydration..............
Blood Pressure...........
PMS.........................

Pain Relief Methods Tried:

Medications Used:

Daily Routine Changes:

Additional Notes:

Begin Time: | End Time: | Duration:

Suggestions For Next Time:

| Mon | Tue | Wed | Thu | Fri | Sat | Sun | Date: | Temp: |

Locations of Pain:

Weather Outside:

Notes:

Pain Tolerance Level:

Triggers:
Eye Strain...............
Bright Lights...............
Loud Sounds...............
Strong Smells...............
Home Stress...............
Driving Stress...............
Work Stress...............
Caffeine...............
Alcohol...............
Hunger...............
Food Choice...............
Oversleep...............
Lack of Sleep...............
Illness...............
Allergies...............
Exertion...............
Dehydration...............
Blood Pressure...........
PMS...............

Pain Relief Methods Tried:

Medications Used:

Daily Routine Changes:

Additional Notes:

Begin Time:

End Time:

Duration:

Suggestions For Next Time:

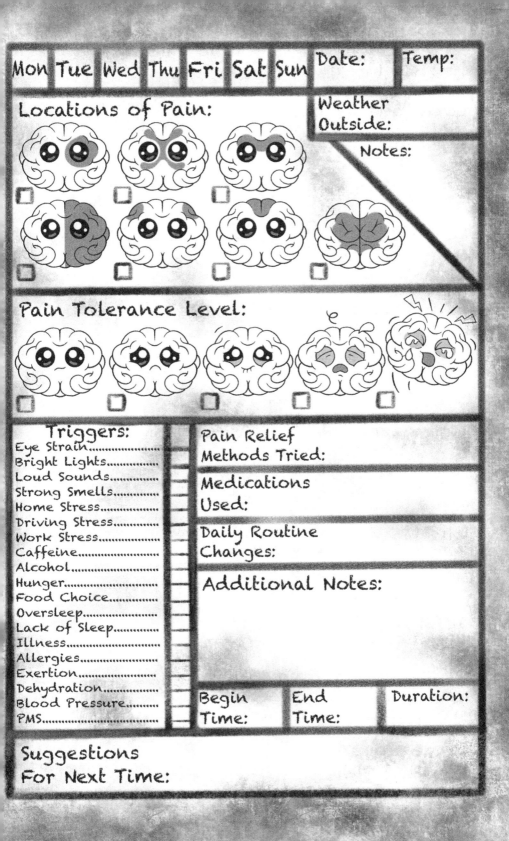

| Mon | Tue | Wed | Thu | Fri | Sat | Sun | Date: | Temp: |

Locations of Pain:

Weather Outside:

Notes:

Pain Tolerance Level:

Triggers:

Eye Strain..................
Bright Lights...............
Loud Sounds..............
Strong Smells.............
Home Stress................
Driving Stress............
Work Stress.................
Caffeine......................
Alcohol........................
Hunger.........................
Food Choice..............
Oversleep....................
Lack of Sleep.............
Illness.........................
Allergies.....................
Exertion.......................
Dehydration................
Blood Pressure...........
PMS.............................

Pain Relief
Methods Tried:

Medications
Used:

Daily Routine
Changes:

Additional Notes:

Begin
Time:

End
Time:

Duration:

Suggestions
For Next Time:

| Mon | Tue | Wed | Thu | Fri | Sat | Sun | Date: | Temp: |

Locations of Pain:

Weather Outside:

Notes:

Pain Tolerance Level:

Triggers:
Eye Strain...............
Bright Lights...............
Loud Sounds...............
Strong Smells...............
Home Stress...............
Driving Stress...............
Work Stress...............
Caffeine...............
Alcohol...............
Hunger...............
Food Choice...............
Oversleep...............
Lack of Sleep...............
Illness...............
Allergies...............
Exertion...............
Dehydration...............
Blood Pressure...............
PMS...............

Pain Relief Methods Tried:

Medications Used:

Daily Routine Changes:

Additional Notes:

Begin Time:

End Time:

Duration:

Suggestions For Next Time:

| Mon | Tue | Wed | Thu | Fri | Sat | Sun | Date: | Temp: |

Locations of Pain:

Weather
Outside:

Notes:

Pain Tolerance Level:

Triggers:

Eye Strain...................
Bright Lights..............
Loud Sounds...............
Strong Smells.............
Home Stress...............
Driving Stress............
Work Stress...............
Caffeine.....................
Alcohol......................
Hunger.......................
Food Choice...............
Oversleep...................
Lack of Sleep.............
Illness........................
Allergies....................
Exertion.....................
Dehydration...............
Blood Pressure..........
PMS...........................

Pain Relief
Methods Tried:

Medications
Used:

Daily Routine
Changes:

Additional Notes:

| Begin Time: | End Time: | Duration: |

Suggestions
For Next Time:

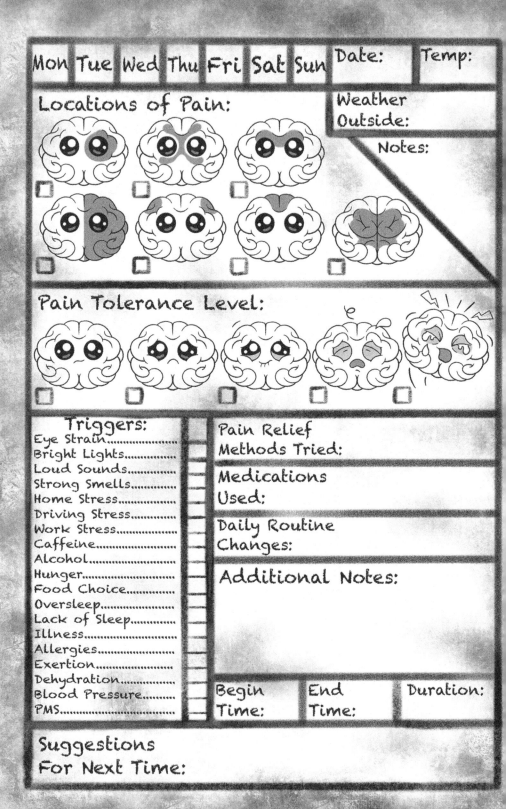

Mon Tue Wed Thu Fri Sat Sun | Date: | Temp:

Locations of Pain:

Weather Outside:

Notes:

Pain Tolerance Level:

Triggers:
Eye Strain................
Bright Lights................
Loud Sounds................
Strong Smells................
Home Stress................
Driving Stress................
Work Stress................
Caffeine................
Alcohol................
Hunger................
Food Choice................
Oversleep................
Lack of Sleep................
Illness................
Allergies................
Exertion................
Dehydration................
Blood Pressure................
PMS................

Pain Relief Methods Tried:

Medications Used:

Daily Routine Changes:

Additional Notes:

Begin Time: | End Time: | Duration:

Suggestions For Next Time:

Mon Tue Wed Thu Fri Sat Sun

Date:

Temp:

Locations of Pain:

Weather Outside:

Notes:

Pain Tolerance Level:

Triggers:

Eye Strain......................
Bright Lights...................
Loud Sounds..................
Strong Smells.................
Home Stress...................
Driving Stress.................
Work Stress...................
Caffeine.......................
Alcohol.........................
Hunger.........................
Food Choice..................
Oversleep......................
Lack of Sleep.................
Illness..........................
Allergies.......................
Exertion........................
Dehydration...................
Blood Pressure..............
PMS.............................

Pain Relief
Methods Tried:

Medications
Used:

Daily Routine
Changes:

Additional Notes:

Begin
Time:

End
Time:

Duration:

Suggestions
For Next Time:

| Mon | Tue | Wed | Thu | Fri | Sat | Sun | Date: | Temp: |

Locations of Pain:

Weather Outside:

Notes:

Pain Tolerance Level:

Triggers:

Eye Strain..................
Bright Lights...............
Loud Sounds...............
Strong Smells..............
Home Stress................
Driving Stress.............
Work Stress.................
Caffeine.....................
Alcohol......................
Hunger.......................
Food Choice...............
Oversleep...................
Lack of Sleep.............
Illness.......................
Allergies....................
Exertion.....................
Dehydration................
Blood Pressure..........
PMS...........................

Pain Relief
Methods Tried:

Medications
Used:

Daily Routine
Changes:

Additional Notes:

Begin
Time:

End
Time:

Duration:

Suggestions
For Next Time:

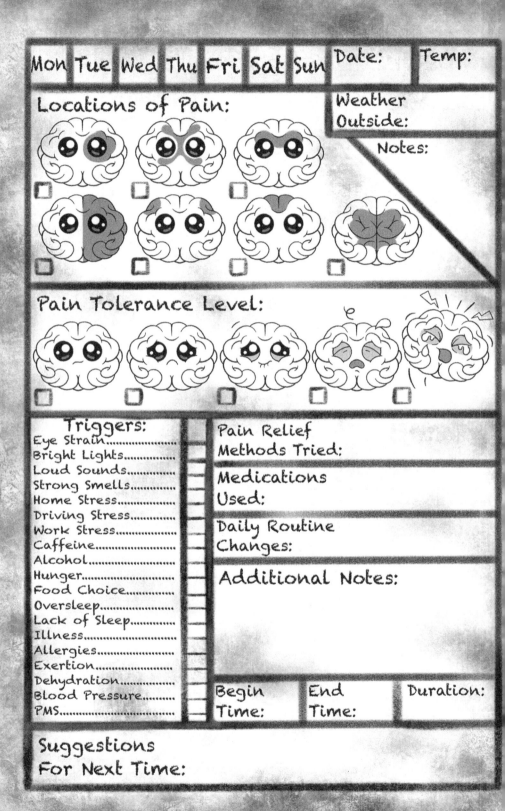

| Mon | Tue | Wed | Thu | Fri | Sat | Sun | Date: | Temp: |

Locations of Pain:

Weather Outside:

Notes:

Pain Tolerance Level:

Triggers:

Eye Strain................
Bright Lights...............
Loud Sounds..............
Strong Smells.............
Home Stress..............
Driving Stress...........
Work Stress..............
Caffeine.....................
Alcohol......................
Hunger......................
Food Choice...............
Oversleep..................
Lack of Sleep..............
Illness......................
Allergies....................
Exertion....................
Dehydration...............
Blood Pressure..........
PMS.........................

Pain Relief Methods Tried:

Medications Used:

Daily Routine Changes:

Additional Notes:

| Begin Time: | End Time: | Duration: |

Suggestions For Next Time:

| Mon | Tue | Wed | Thu | Fri | Sat | Sun | Date: | Temp: |

Locations of Pain:

Weather Outside:

Notes:

Pain Tolerance Level:

Triggers:

Eye Strain...............
Bright Lights..............
Loud Sounds..............
Strong Smells.............
Home Stress..............
Driving Stress.............
Work Stress...............
Caffeine...................
Alcohol.....................
Hunger.....................
Food Choice..............
Oversleep..................
Lack of Sleep.............
Illness......................
Allergies...................
Exertion....................
Dehydration...............
Blood Pressure..........
PMS........................

Pain Relief Methods Tried:

Medications Used:

Daily Routine Changes:

Additional Notes:

| Begin Time: | End Time: | Duration: |

Suggestions For Next Time:

| Mon | Tue | Wed | Thu | Fri | Sat | Sun | Date: | Temp: |

Locations of Pain:

Weather Outside:

Notes:

Pain Tolerance Level:

Triggers:
Eye Strain...........................
Bright Lights...................
Loud Sounds.....................
Strong Smells.................
Home Stress.....................
Driving Stress...............
Work Stress.....................
Caffeine.............................
Alcohol...............................
Hunger...............................
Food Choice...................
Oversleep.........................
Lack of Sleep.................
Illness................................
Allergies...........................
Exertion............................
Dehydration....................
Blood Pressure...........
PMS......................................

Pain Relief Methods Tried:

Medications Used:

Daily Routine Changes:

Additional Notes:

Begin Time:

End Time:

Duration:

Suggestions For Next Time:

| Mon | Tue | Wed | Thu | Fri | Sat | Sun | Date: | Temp: |

Locations of Pain:

Weather
Outside:

Notes:

Pain Tolerance Level:

Triggers:
Eye Strain................
Bright Lights.............
Loud Sounds..............
Strong Smells.............
Home Stress..............
Driving Stress............
Work Stress..............
Caffeine..................
Alcohol...................
Hunger....................
Food Choice..............
Oversleep.................
Lack of Sleep............
Illness...................
Allergies.................
Exertion..................
Dehydration..............
Blood Pressure..........
PMS......................

Pain Relief
Methods Tried:

Medications
Used:

Daily Routine
Changes:

Additional Notes:

Begin
Time:

End
Time:

Duration:

**Suggestions
For Next Time:**

Mon	Tue	Wed	Thu	Fri	Sat	Sun	Date:	Temp:

Locations of Pain:

Weather Outside:

Notes:

Pain Tolerance Level:

Triggers:

Eye Strain.....................
Bright Lights.................
Loud Sounds.................
Strong Smells...............
Home Stress.................
Driving Stress...............
Work Stress...................
Caffeine.........................
Alcohol..........................
Hunger...........................
Food Choice..................
Oversleep......................
Lack of Sleep.................
Illness............................
Allergies........................
Exertion.........................
Dehydration...................
Blood Pressure.............
PMS...............................

Pain Relief Methods Tried:

Medications Used:

Daily Routine Changes:

Additional Notes:

Begin Time:	End Time:	Duration:

Suggestions For Next Time:

| Mon | Tue | Wed | Thu | Fri | Sat | Sun | Date: | Temp: |

Locations of Pain:

Weather Outside:

Notes:

☐   ☐   ☐

☐   ☐   ☐   ☐

Pain Tolerance Level:

☐   ☐   ☐   ☐   ☐

Triggers:

Eye Strain.....................
Bright Lights................
Loud Sounds................
Strong Smells...............
Home Stress.................
Driving Stress..............
Work Stress..................
Caffeine........................
Alcohol..........................
Hunger...........................
Food Choice.................
Oversleep......................
Lack of Sleep...............
Illness............................
Allergies........................
Exertion.........................
Dehydration..................
Blood Pressure...........
PMS................................

Pain Relief Methods Tried:

Medications Used:

Daily Routine Changes:

Additional Notes:

| Begin Time: | End Time: | Duration: |

Suggestions For Next Time:

| Mon | Tue | Wed | Thu | Fri | Sat | Sun | Date: | Temp: |

Locations of Pain:

Weather Outside:

Notes:

Pain Tolerance Level:

Triggers:
Eye Strain.....................
Bright Lights................
Loud Sounds................
Strong Smells..............
Home Stress.................
Driving Stress..............
Work Stress..................
Caffeine........................
Alcohol..........................
Hunger..........................
Food Choice................
Oversleep.....................
Lack of Sleep..............
Illness...........................
Allergies.......................
Exertion.......................
Dehydration................
Blood Pressure..........
PMS...............................

Pain Relief Methods Tried:

Medications Used:

Daily Routine Changes:

Additional Notes:

Begin Time:

End Time:

Duration:

Suggestions For Next Time:

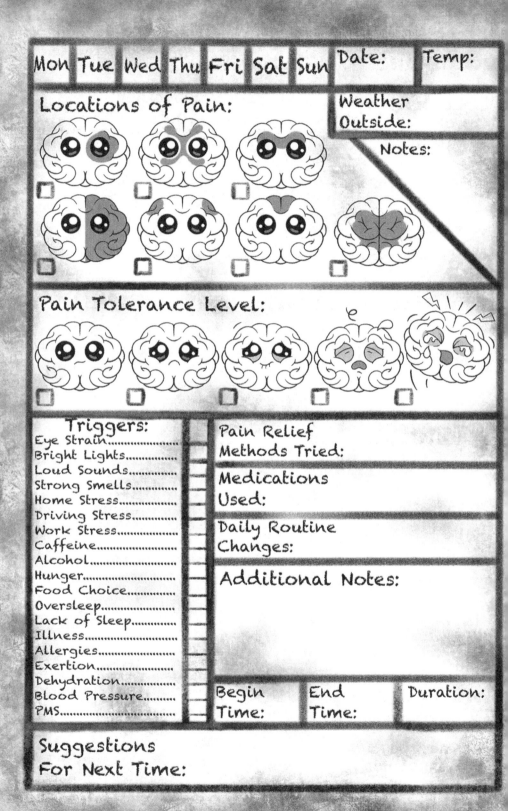

Mon	Tue	Wed	Thu	Fri	Sat	Sun	Date:	Temp:

Locations of Pain:

Weather
Outside:

Notes:

Pain Tolerance Level:

Triggers:

Eye Strain...............
Bright Lights..............
Loud Sounds..............
Strong Smells.............
Home Stress..............
Driving Stress...........
Work Stress..................
Caffeine.....................
Alcohol......................
Hunger.......................
Food Choice..............
Oversleep..................
Lack of Sleep.............
Illness.......................
Allergies....................
Exertion....................
Dehydration...............
Blood Pressure..........
PMS...........................

Pain Relief
Methods Tried:

Medications
Used:

Daily Routine
Changes:

Additional Notes:

Begin Time:	End Time:	Duration:

Suggestions
For Next Time:

| Mon | Tue | Wed | Thu | Fri | Sat | Sun | Date: | Temp: |

Locations of Pain:

Weather
Outside:

Notes:

Pain Tolerance Level:

Triggers:

Eye Strain..............
Bright Lights..............
Loud Sounds..............
Strong Smells..............
Home Stress..............
Driving Stress..............
Work Stress..............
Caffeine..............
Alcohol..............
Hunger..............
Food Choice..............
Oversleep..............
Lack of Sleep..............
Illness..............
Allergies..............
Exertion..............
Dehydration..............
Blood Pressure..........
PMS..............

Pain Relief
Methods Tried:

Medications
Used:

Daily Routine
Changes:

Additional Notes:

| Begin Time: | End Time: | Duration: |

Suggestions
For Next Time:

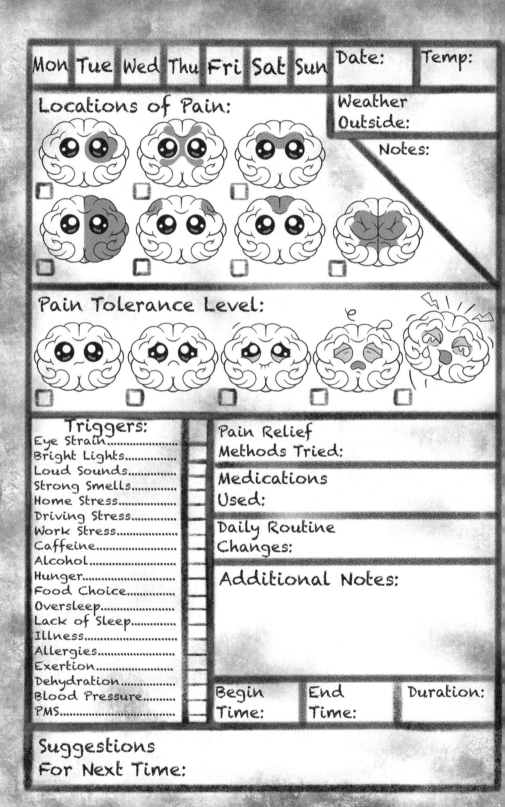

Mon Tue Wed Thu Fri Sat Sun Date: Temp:

Locations of Pain:

Weather Outside:

Notes:

Pain Tolerance Level:

Triggers:
Eye Strain................
Bright Lights.............
Loud Sounds.............
Strong Smells...........
Home Stress.............
Driving Stress...........
Work Stress.............
Caffeine...................
Alcohol....................
Hunger.....................
Food Choice.............
Oversleep.................
Lack of Sleep...........
Illness.....................
Allergies..................
Exertion...................
Dehydration.............
Blood Pressure.........
PMS........................

Pain Relief
Methods Tried:

Medications
Used:

Daily Routine
Changes:

Additional Notes:

Begin
Time:

End
Time:

Duration:

Suggestions
For Next Time:

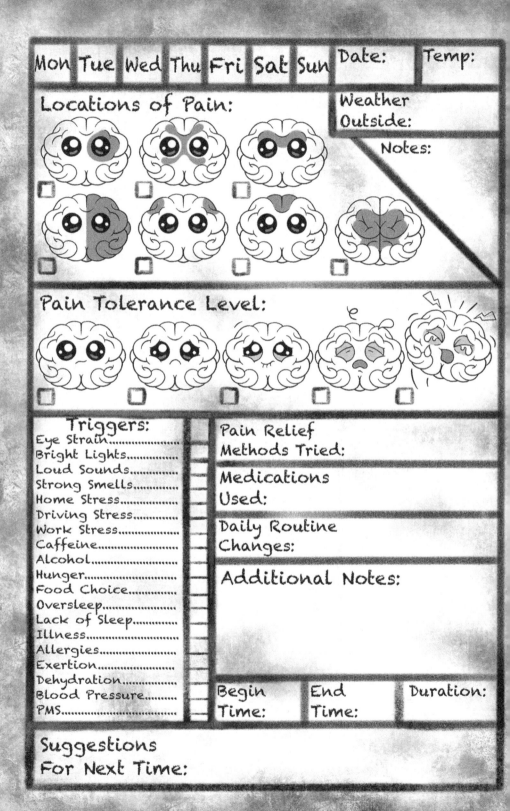

| Mon | Tue | Wed | Thu | Fri | Sat | Sun | Date: | Temp: |

Locations of Pain:

☐ ☐ ☐
☐ ☐ ☐ ☐

Weather Outside:

Notes:

Pain Tolerance Level:

☐ ☐ ☐ ☐ ☐

Triggers:

Eye Strain.........................
Bright Lights....................
Loud Sounds....................
Strong Smells...................
Home Stress.....................
Driving Stress...................
Work Stress......................
Caffeine............................
Alcohol.............................
Hunger..............................
Food Choice....................
Oversleep.........................
Lack of Sleep...................
Illness...............................
Allergies...........................
Exertion............................
Dehydration.....................
Blood Pressure................
PMS...................................

Pain Relief Methods Tried:

Medications Used:

Daily Routine Changes:

Additional Notes:

| Begin Time: | End Time: | Duration: |

Suggestions For Next Time:

| Mon | Tue | Wed | Thu | Fri | Sat | Sun | Date: | Temp: |

Locations of Pain:

☐ ☐ ☐

☐ ☐ ☐ ☐

Weather Outside:

Notes:

Pain Tolerance Level:

☐ ☐ ☐ ☐ ☐

Triggers:
Eye Strain.................
Bright Lights.............
Loud Sounds.............
Strong Smells.............
Home Stress..............
Driving Stress...........
Work Stress..............
Caffeine...................
Alcohol....................
Hunger....................
Food Choice..............
Oversleep.................
Lack of Sleep............
Illness.....................
Allergies..................
Exertion...................
Dehydration..............
Blood Pressure..........
PMS........................

Pain Relief Methods Tried:

Medications Used:

Daily Routine Changes:

Additional Notes:

Begin Time:

End Time:

Duration:

Suggestions For Next Time:

| Mon | Tue | Wed | Thu | Fri | Sat | Sun | Date: | Temp: |

Locations of Pain:

Weather Outside:

Notes:

Pain Tolerance Level:

Triggers:
Eye Strain..................
Bright Lights..............
Loud Sounds..............
Strong Smells.............
Home Stress...............
Driving Stress.............
Work Stress...............
Caffeine....................
Alcohol......................
Hunger.......................
Food Choice...............
Oversleep...................
Lack of Sleep..............
Illness........................
Allergies.....................
Exertion......................
Dehydration...............
Blood Pressure...........
PMS..........................

Pain Relief Methods Tried:

Medications Used:

Daily Routine Changes:

Additional Notes:

Begin Time:

End Time:

Duration:

Suggestions For Next Time:

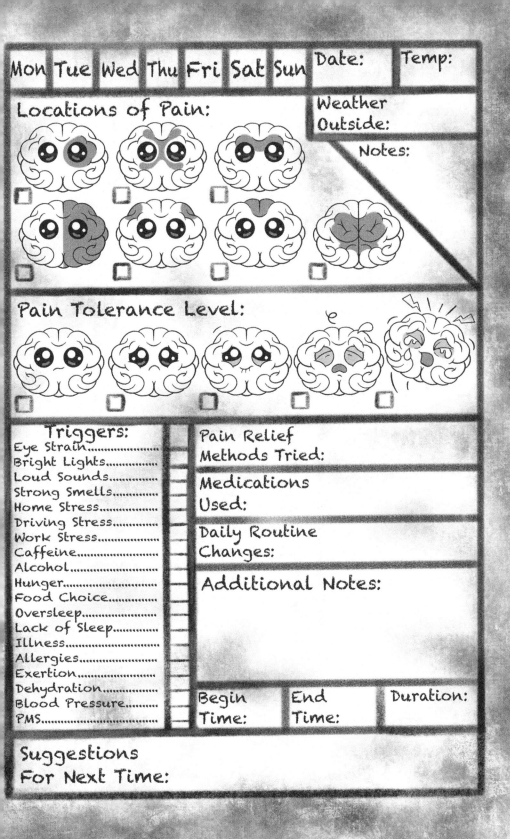

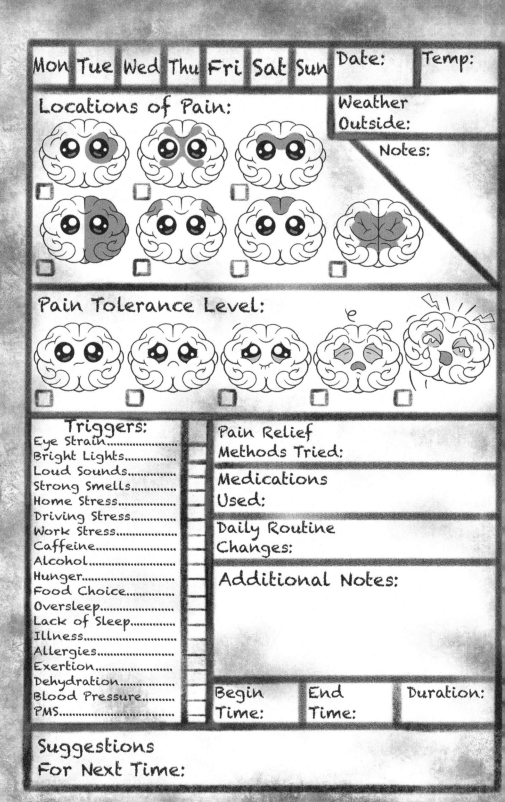

| Mon | Tue | Wed | Thu | Fri | Sat | Sun | Date: | Temp: |

Locations of Pain:

Weather Outside:

Notes:

Pain Tolerance Level:

Triggers:

Eye Strain..............
Bright Lights..............
Loud Sounds..............
Strong Smells..............
Home Stress..............
Driving Stress..............
Work Stress..............
Caffeine..............
Alcohol..............
Hunger..............
Food Choice..............
Oversleep..............
Lack of Sleep..............
Illness..............
Allergies..............
Exertion..............
Dehydration..............
Blood Pressure..........
PMS..............

Pain Relief Methods Tried:

Medications Used:

Daily Routine Changes:

Additional Notes:

| Begin Time: | End Time: | Duration: |

Suggestions For Next Time:

| Mon | Tue | Wed | Thu | Fri | Sat | Sun | Date: | Temp: |

Locations of Pain:

Weather
Outside:

Notes:

Pain Tolerance Level:

Triggers:

Eye Strain.......................
Bright Lights..................
Loud Sounds..................
Strong Smells...............
Home Stress...................
Driving Stress...............
Work Stress...................
Caffeine..........................
Alcohol...........................
Hunger............................
Food Choice..................
Oversleep.......................
Lack of Sleep...............
Illness.............................
Allergies.........................
Exertion..........................
Dehydration...................
Blood Pressure...........
PMS..................................

Pain Relief
Methods Tried:

Medications
Used:

Daily Routine
Changes:

Additional Notes:

Begin
Time:

End
Time:

Duration:

**Suggestions
For Next Time:**

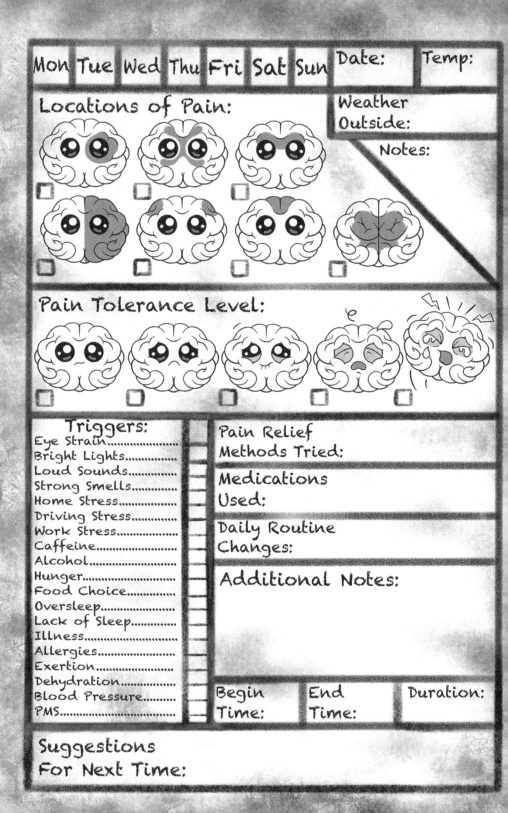

Mon	Tue	Wed	Thu	Fri	Sat	Sun	Date:	Temp:

Locations of Pain:

Weather Outside:

Notes:

Pain Tolerance Level:

Triggers:

Eye Strain.....................
Bright Lights..................
Loud Sounds..................
Strong Smells................
Home Stress..................
Driving Stress...............
Work Stress...................
Caffeine........................
Alcohol.........................
Hunger..........................
Food Choice..................
Oversleep......................
Lack of Sleep...............
Illness..........................
Allergies.......................
Exertion........................
Dehydration..................
Blood Pressure.............
PMS..............................

Pain Relief Methods Tried:

Medications Used:

Daily Routine Changes:

Additional Notes:

Begin Time:

End Time:

Duration:

Suggestions For Next Time:

| Mon | Tue | Wed | Thu | Fri | Sat | Sun | Date: | Temp: |

Locations of Pain:

Weather
Outside:

Notes:

☐ ☐ ☐

☐ ☐ ☐

Pain Tolerance Level:

☐ ☐ ☐ ☐ ☐

Triggers:
Eye Strain...............
Bright Lights...............
Loud Sounds...............
Strong Smells...............
Home Stress...............
Driving Stress...............
Work Stress...............
Caffeine...............
Alcohol...............
Hunger...............
Food Choice...............
Oversleep...............
Lack of Sleep...............
Illness...............
Allergies...............
Exertion...............
Dehydration...............
Blood Pressure...........
PMS...............

Pain Relief
Methods Tried:

Medications
Used:

Daily Routine
Changes:

Additional Notes:

| Begin Time: | End Time: | Duration: |

Suggestions
For Next Time:

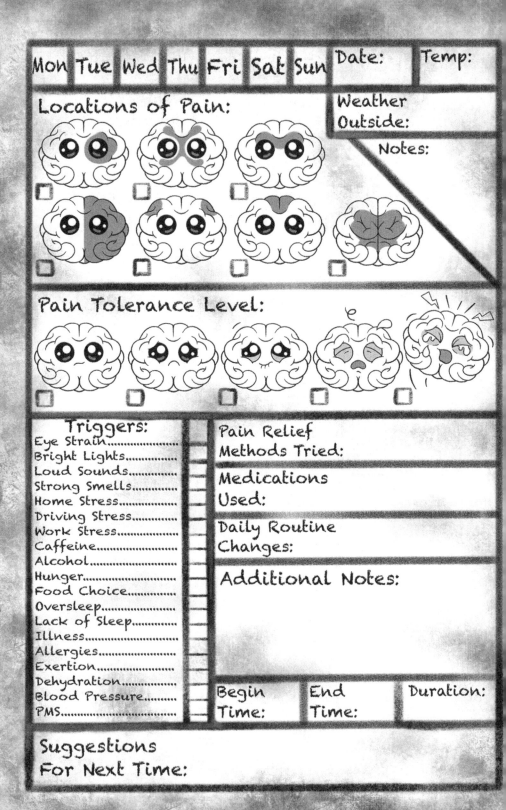

Mon | Tue | Wed | Thu | Fri | Sat | Sun | Date: | Temp:

Locations of Pain:

Weather Outside:

Notes:

Pain Tolerance Level:

Triggers:
Eye Strain...................
Bright Lights...............
Loud Sounds...............
Strong Smells.............
Home Stress...............
Driving Stress.............
Work Stress................
Caffeine.......................
Alcohol........................
Hunger.........................
Food Choice..............
Oversleep....................
Lack of Sleep.............
Illness.........................
Allergies......................
Exertion......................
Dehydration...............
Blood Pressure..........
PMS.............................

Pain Relief Methods Tried:

Medications Used:

Daily Routine Changes:

Additional Notes:

Begin Time: | End Time: | Duration:

Suggestions For Next Time:

Mon	Tue	Wed	Thu	Fri	Sat	Sun	Date:	Temp:

Locations of Pain:

Weather Outside:

Notes:

Pain Tolerance Level:

Triggers:
Eye Strain.....................
Bright Lights................
Loud Sounds................
Strong Smells..............
Home Stress.................
Driving Stress..............
Work Stress..................
Caffeine........................
Alcohol..........................
Hunger..........................
Food Choice.................
Oversleep......................
Lack of Sleep...............
Illness...........................
Allergies........................
Exertion........................
Dehydration.................
Blood Pressure............
PMS...............................

Pain Relief
Methods Tried:

Medications
Used:

Daily Routine
Changes:

Additional Notes:

Begin Time: | End Time: | Duration:

Suggestions
For Next Time:

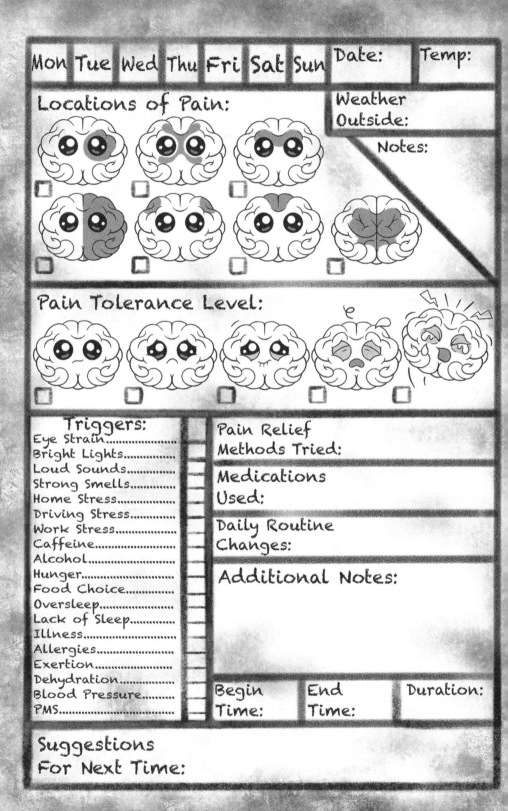

| Mon | Tue | Wed | Thu | Fri | Sat | Sun | Date: | Temp: |

Locations of Pain:

Weather
Outside:

Notes:

Pain Tolerance Level:

Triggers:
Eye Strain......................
Bright Lights................
Loud Sounds.................
Strong Smells...............
Home Stress..................
Driving Stress..............
Work Stress..................
Caffeine.........................
Alcohol..........................
Hunger...........................
Food Choice.................
Oversleep......................
Lack of Sleep...............
Illness............................
Allergies........................
Exertion.........................
Dehydration..................
Blood Pressure...........
PMS................................

Pain Relief
Methods Tried:

Medications
Used:

Daily Routine
Changes:

Additional Notes:

Begin
Time:

End
Time:

Duration:

Suggestions
For Next Time:

| Mon | Tue | Wed | Thu | Fri | Sat | Sun | Date: | Temp: |

Locations of Pain:

Weather Outside:

Notes:

Pain Tolerance Level:

Triggers:
Eye Strain..................
Bright Lights..............
Loud Sounds...............
Strong Smells.............
Home Stress................
Driving Stress.............
Work Stress................
Caffeine.....................
Alcohol......................
Hunger.......................
Food Choice...............
Oversleep...................
Lack of Sleep.............
Illness.......................
Allergies....................
Exertion.....................
Dehydration...............
Blood Pressure...........
PMS...........................

Pain Relief Methods Tried:

Medications Used:

Daily Routine Changes:

Additional Notes:

Begin Time:

End Time:

Duration:

Suggestions For Next Time:

| Mon | Tue | Wed | Thu | Fri | Sat | Sun | Date: | Temp: |

Locations of Pain:

Weather Outside:

Notes:

☐ ☐ ☐

☐ ☐ ☐ ☐

Pain Tolerance Level:

☐ ☐ ☐ ☐ ☐

Triggers:

Eye Strain.........................
Bright Lights..................
Loud Sounds.................
Strong Smells...............
Home Stress.................
Driving Stress...............
Work Stress...................
Caffeine..........................
Alcohol............................
Hunger.............................
Food Choice.................
Oversleep........................
Lack of Sleep...............
Illness.............................
Allergies.........................
Exertion..........................
Dehydration..................
Blood Pressure...........
PMS...................................

Pain Relief
Methods Tried:

Medications
Used:

Daily Routine
Changes:

Additional Notes:

Begin
Time:

End
Time:

Duration:

Suggestions
For Next Time:

Mon	Tue	Wed	Thu	Fri	Sat	Sun	Date:	Temp:

Locations of Pain:

Weather
Outside:

Notes:

Pain Tolerance Level:

Triggers:

Eye Strain.....................
Bright Lights.................
Loud Sounds...............
Strong Smells..............
Home Stress.................
Driving Stress...............
Work Stress...................
Caffeine.........................
Alcohol..........................
Hunger..........................
Food Choice.................
Oversleep......................
Lack of Sleep..............
Illness............................
Allergies.......................
Exertion........................
Dehydration................
Blood Pressure..........
PMS.................................

Pain Relief Methods Tried:

Medications Used:

Daily Routine Changes:

Additional Notes:

Begin Time:	End Time:	Duration:

Suggestions For Next Time:

| Mon | Tue | Wed | Thu | Fri | Sat | Sun | Date: | Temp: |

Locations of Pain:

Weather Outside:

Notes:

Pain Tolerance Level:

Triggers:

Eye Strain.............
Bright Lights...........
Loud Sounds............
Strong Smells...........
Home Stress.............
Driving Stress..........
Work Stress.............
Caffeine................
Alcohol................
Hunger.................
Food Choice............
Oversleep..............
Lack of Sleep..........
Illness................
Allergies..............
Exertion...............
Dehydration............
Blood Pressure.........
PMS....................

Pain Relief Methods Tried:

Medications Used:

Daily Routine Changes:

Additional Notes:

| Begin Time: | End Time: | Duration: |

Suggestions For Next Time:

| Mon | Tue | Wed | Thu | Fri | Sat | Sun | Date: | Temp: |

Locations of Pain:

Weather
Outside:

Notes:

Pain Tolerance Level:

Triggers:

Eye Strain...............
Bright Lights.............
Loud Sounds...............
Strong Smells.............
Home Stress...............
Driving Stress...........
Work Stress..............
Caffeine.................
Alcohol..................
Hunger...................
Food Choice..............
Oversleep................
Lack of Sleep............
Illness..................
Allergies................
Exertion.................
Dehydration..............
Blood Pressure...........
PMS......................

Pain Relief
Methods Tried:

Medications
Used:

Daily Routine
Changes:

Additional Notes:

| Begin Time: | End Time: | Duration: |

Suggestions For Next Time:

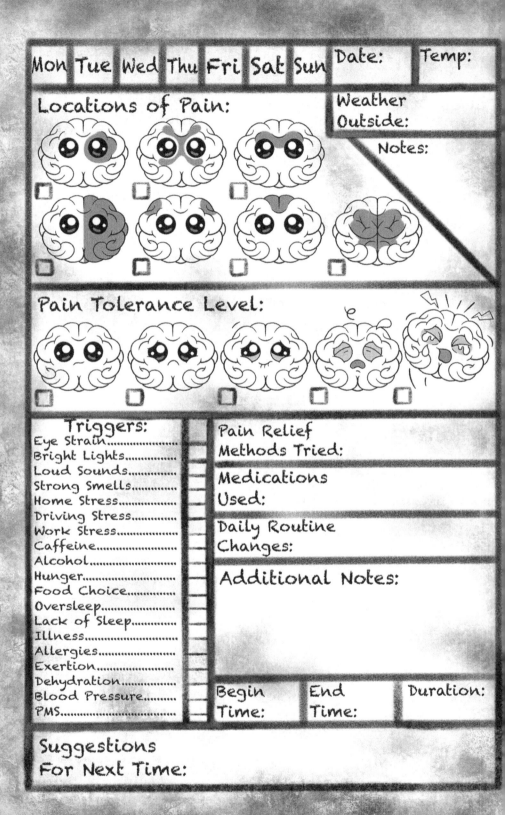

Mon	Tue	Wed	Thu	Fri	Sat	Sun	Date:	Temp:

Locations of Pain:

Weather
Outside:

Notes:

☐ ☐ ☐

☐ ☐ ☐ ☐

Pain Tolerance Level:

☐ ☐ ☐ ☐ ☐

Triggers:

Eye Strain.....................
Bright Lights................
Loud Sounds................
Strong Smells...............
Home Stress.................
Driving Stress...............
Work Stress..................
Caffeine.......................
Alcohol........................
Hunger.........................
Food Choice.................
Oversleep.....................
Lack of Sleep...............
Illness.........................
Allergies.......................
Exertion.......................
Dehydration.................
Blood Pressure............
PMS............................

Pain Relief
Methods Tried:

Medications
Used:

Daily Routine
Changes:

Additional Notes:

Begin Time:	End Time:	Duration:

Suggestions For Next Time:

| Mon | Tue | Wed | Thu | Fri | Sat | Sun | Date: | Temp: |

Locations of Pain:

Weather Outside:

Notes:

☐ ☐ ☐

☐ ☐ ☐ ☐

Pain Tolerance Level:

☐ ☐ ☐ ☐ ☐

Triggers:

Eye Strain...........................
Bright Lights.....................
Loud Sounds.....................
Strong Smells...................
Home Stress......................
Driving Stress...................
Work Stress......................
Caffeine...............................
Alcohol...............................
Hunger...............................
Food Choice.....................
Oversleep...........................
Lack of Sleep...................
Illness.................................
Allergies.............................
Exertion.............................
Dehydration.....................
Blood Pressure...............
PMS.....................................

Pain Relief
Methods Tried:

Medications
Used:

Daily Routine
Changes:

Additional Notes:

| Begin Time: | End Time: | Duration: |

Suggestions For Next Time:

| Mon | Tue | Wed | Thu | Fri | Sat | Sun | Date: | Temp: |

Locations of Pain:

Weather
Outside:

Notes:

Pain Tolerance Level:

Triggers:

Eye Strain..................
Bright Lights.............
Loud Sounds.............
Strong Smells...........
Home Stress.............
Driving Stress...........
Work Stress...............
Caffeine.....................
Alcohol......................
Hunger.......................
Food Choice..............
Oversleep...................
Lack of Sleep............
Illness........................
Allergies....................
Exertion.....................
Dehydration..............
Blood Pressure..........
PMS.............................

Pain Relief
Methods Tried:

Medications
Used:

Daily Routine
Changes:

Additional Notes:

Begin
Time:

End
Time:

Duration:

Suggestions
For Next Time:

Mon	Tue	Wed	Thu	Fri	Sat	Sun	Date:	Temp:

Locations of Pain:

Weather Outside:

Notes:

Pain Tolerance Level:

Triggers:

Eye Strain..................
Bright Lights..............
Loud Sounds..............
Strong Smells.............
Home Stress..............
Driving Stress............
Work Stress................
Caffeine......................
Alcohol.......................
Hunger.......................
Food Choice..............
Oversleep...................
Lack of Sleep............
Illness........................
Allergies.....................
Exertion......................
Dehydration..............
Blood Pressure..........
PMS...........................

Pain Relief Methods Tried:

Medications Used:

Daily Routine Changes:

Additional Notes:

Begin Time:	End Time:	Duration:

Suggestions For Next Time:

| Mon | Tue | Wed | Thu | Fri | Sat | Sun | Date: | Temp: |

Locations of Pain:

Weather Outside:

Notes:

Pain Tolerance Level:

Triggers:

Eye Strain.................
Bright Lights...............
Loud Sounds..............
Strong Smells.............
Home Stress...............
Driving Stress............
Work Stress................
Caffeine.....................
Alcohol......................
Hunger.......................
Food Choice..............
Oversleep..................
Lack of Sleep............
Illness.......................
Allergies....................
Exertion.....................
Dehydration..............
Blood Pressure..........
PMS..........................

Pain Relief Methods Tried:

Medications Used:

Daily Routine Changes:

Additional Notes:

Begin Time:

End Time:

Duration:

Suggestions For Next Time:

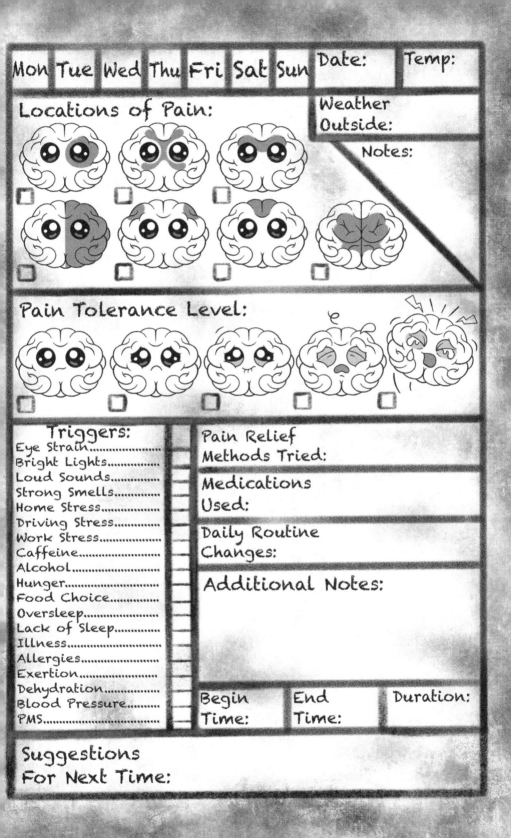

| Mon | Tue | Wed | Thu | Fri | Sat | Sun | Date: | Temp: |

Locations of Pain:

Weather Outside:

Notes:

Pain Tolerance Level:

Triggers:

Eye Strain......................
Bright Lights.................
Loud Sounds.................
Strong Smells...............
Home Stress.................
Driving Stress...............
Work Stress.................
Caffeine........................
Alcohol.........................
Hunger.........................
Food Choice.................
Oversleep......................
Lack of Sleep...............
Illness...........................
Allergies.......................
Exertion........................
Dehydration.................
Blood Pressure.............
PMS..............................

Pain Relief Methods Tried:

Medications Used:

Daily Routine Changes:

Additional Notes:

| Begin Time: | End Time: | Duration: |

Suggestions For Next Time:

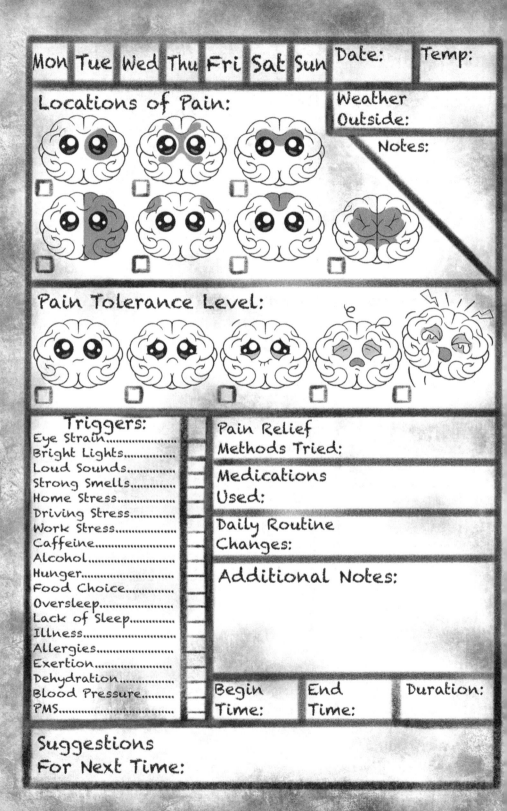

Mon | Tue | Wed | Thu | Fri | Sat | Sun | Date: | Temp:

Locations of Pain:

Weather Outside:

Notes:

Pain Tolerance Level:

Triggers:
Eye Strain...............
Bright Lights...............
Loud Sounds...............
Strong Smells...............
Home Stress...............
Driving Stress...............
Work Stress...............
Caffeine...............
Alcohol...............
Hunger...............
Food Choice...............
Oversleep...............
Lack of Sleep...............
Illness...............
Allergies...............
Exertion...............
Dehydration...............
Blood Pressure...........
PMS...............

Pain Relief
Methods Tried:

Medications
Used:

Daily Routine
Changes:

Additional Notes:

Begin
Time:

End
Time:

Duration:

Suggestions
For Next Time:

| Mon | Tue | Wed | Thu | Fri | Sat | Sun | Date: | Temp: |

Locations of Pain:

Weather Outside:

Notes:

☐ ☐ ☐

☐ ☐ ☐ ☐

Pain Tolerance Level:

☐ ☐ ☐ ☐ ☐

Triggers:

Eye Strain.............
Bright Lights..............
Loud Sounds.............
Strong Smells...............
Home Stress...............
Driving Stress............
Work Stress.............
Caffeine...............
Alcohol.................
Hunger....................
Food Choice..............
Oversleep.................
Lack of Sleep............
Illness...................
Allergies...............
Exertion..............
Dehydration................
Blood Pressure..........
PMS.......................

Pain Relief
Methods Tried:

Medications
Used:

Daily Routine
Changes:

Additional Notes:

| Begin Time: | End Time: | Duration: |

Suggestions For Next Time:

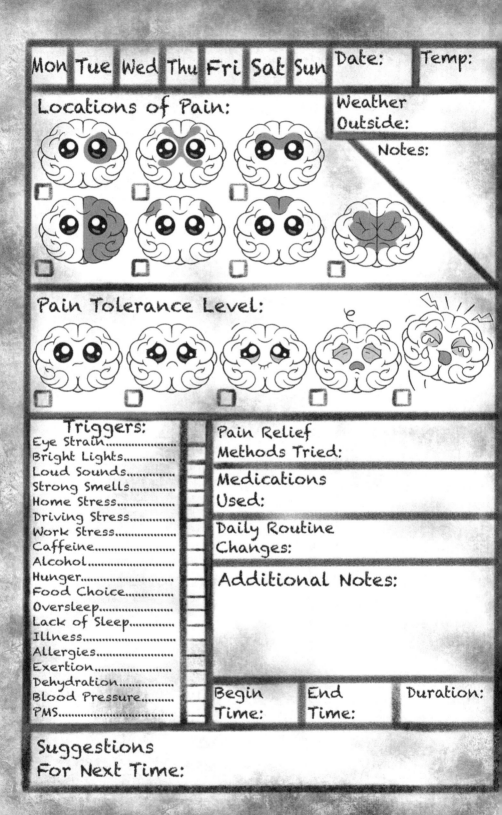

Mon Tue Wed Thu Fri Sat Sun Date: Temp:

Locations of Pain: Weather Outside:

Notes:

Pain Tolerance Level:

Triggers:
Eye Strain..................
Bright Lights..............
Loud Sounds..............
Strong Smells............
Home Stress..............
Driving Stress............
Work Stress...............
Caffeine.....................
Alcohol......................
Hunger.......................
Food Choice..............
Oversleep...................
Lack of Sleep............
Illness.......................
Allergies....................
Exertion.....................
Dehydration...............
Blood Pressure..........
PMS...........................

Pain Relief
Methods Tried:

Medications
Used:

Daily Routine
Changes:

Additional Notes:

Begin
Time:

End
Time:

Duration:

Suggestions
For Next Time:

| Mon | Tue | Wed | Thu | Fri | Sat | Sun | Date: | Temp: |

Locations of Pain:

Weather Outside:

Notes:

Pain Tolerance Level:

Triggers:

Eye Strain...............
Bright Lights...............
Loud Sounds...............
Strong Smells...............
Home Stress...............
Driving Stress...............
Work Stress...............
Caffeine...............
Alcohol...............
Hunger...............
Food Choice...............
Oversleep...............
Lack of Sleep...............
Illness...............
Allergies...............
Exertion...............
Dehydration...............
Blood Pressure...............
PMS...............

Pain Relief Methods Tried:

Medications Used:

Daily Routine Changes:

Additional Notes:

Begin Time:

End Time:

Duration:

Suggestions For Next Time:

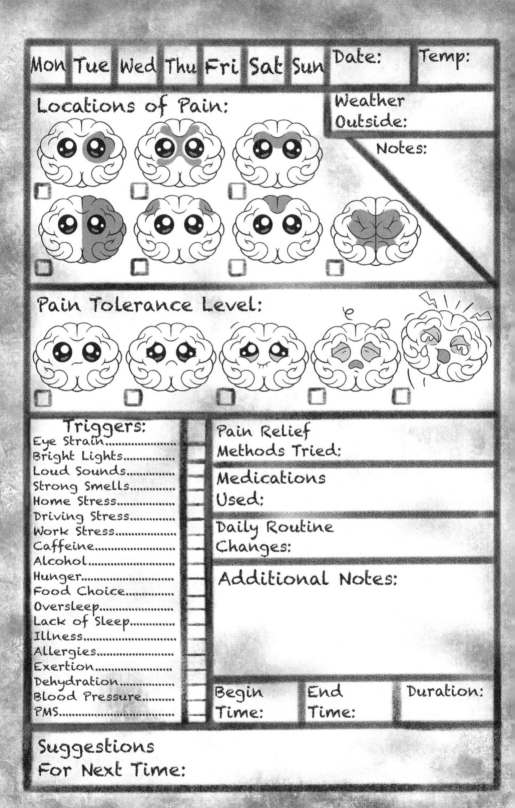

Mon | Tue | Wed | Thu | Fri | Sat | Sun

Date:

Temp:

Locations of Pain:

Weather Outside:

Notes:

Pain Tolerance Level:

Triggers:
Eye Strain.................
Bright Lights..............
Loud Sounds.............
Strong Smells..............
Home Stress................
Driving Stress.............
Work Stress..................
Caffeine.......................
Alcohol..........................
Hunger..........................
Food Choice...............
Oversleep......................
Lack of Sleep.............
Illness...........................
Allergies.......................
Exertion........................
Dehydration................
Blood Pressure..........
PMS................................

Pain Relief Methods Tried:

Medications Used:

Daily Routine Changes:

Additional Notes:

Begin Time:

End Time:

Duration:

Suggestions For Next Time:

| Mon | Tue | Wed | Thu | Fri | Sat | Sun | Date: | Temp: |

Locations of Pain:

Weather Outside:

Notes:

Pain Tolerance Level:

Triggers:

Eye Strain......................
Bright Lights...............
Loud Sounds..............
Strong Smells.............
Home Stress...............
Driving Stress.............
Work Stress.................
Caffeine.......................
Alcohol........................
Hunger........................
Food Choice...............
Oversleep....................
Lack of Sleep.............
Illness.........................
Allergies......................
Exertion......................
Dehydration...............
Blood Pressure..........
PMS.............................

Pain Relief Methods Tried:

Medications Used:

Daily Routine Changes:

Additional Notes:

| Begin Time: | End Time: | Duration: |

Suggestions For Next Time:

| Mon | Tue | Wed | Thu | Fri | Sat | Sun | Date: | Temp: |

Locations of Pain:

Weather Outside:

Notes:

Pain Tolerance Level:

Triggers:

Eye Strain...................
Bright Lights...............
Loud Sounds..............
Strong Smells.............
Home Stress...............
Driving Stress............
Work Stress................
Caffeine......................
Alcohol.......................
Hunger........................
Food Choice...............
Oversleep....................
Lack of Sleep..............
Illness.........................
Allergies......................
Exertion.......................
Dehydration................
Blood Pressure...........
PMS.............................

Pain Relief Methods Tried:

Medications Used:

Daily Routine Changes:

Additional Notes:

Begin Time:

End Time:

Duration:

Suggestions For Next Time:

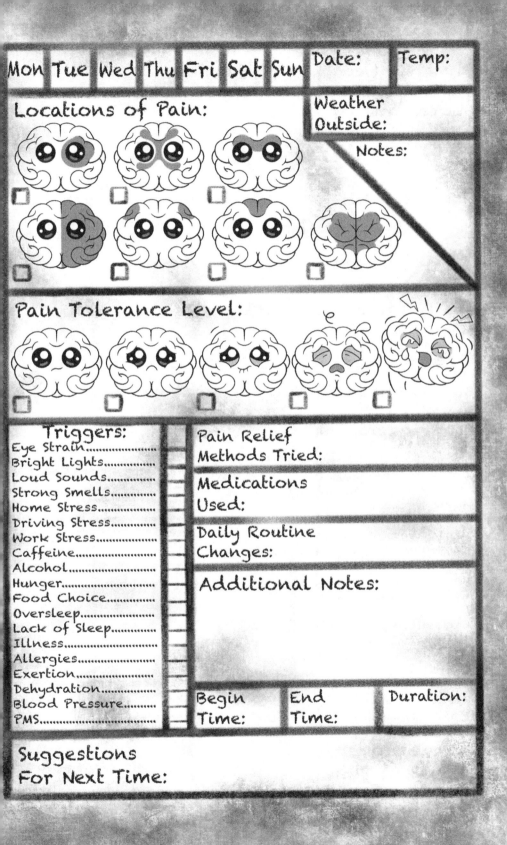

Mon Tue Wed Thu Fri Sat Sun | Date: | Temp:

Weather Outside:

Notes:

Locations of Pain:

Pain Tolerance Level:

Triggers:
Eye Strain..............
Bright Lights..............
Loud Sounds..............
Strong Smells..............
Home Stress..............
Driving Stress..............
Work Stress..............
Caffeine..............
Alcohol..............
Hunger..............
Food Choice..............
Oversleep..............
Lack of Sleep..............
Illness..............
Allergies..............
Exertion..............
Dehydration..............
Blood Pressure..............
PMS..............

Pain Relief Methods Tried:

Medications Used:

Daily Routine Changes:

Additional Notes:

Begin Time: | End Time: | Duration:

Suggestions For Next Time:

| Mon | Tue | Wed | Thu | Fri | Sat | Sun | Date: | Temp: |

Locations of Pain:

Weather Outside:

Notes:

Pain Tolerance Level:

Triggers:
Eye Strain.....................
Bright Lights.................
Loud Sounds.................
Strong Smells...............
Home Stress..................
Driving Stress...............
Work Stress...................
Caffeine........................
Alcohol..........................
Hunger...........................
Food Choice..................
Oversleep......................
Lack of Sleep...............
Illness............................
Allergies........................
Exertion.........................
Dehydration..................
Blood Pressure............
PMS................................

Pain Relief
Methods Tried:

Medications
Used:

Daily Routine
Changes:

Additional Notes:

Begin
Time:

End
Time:

Duration:

Suggestions
For Next Time:

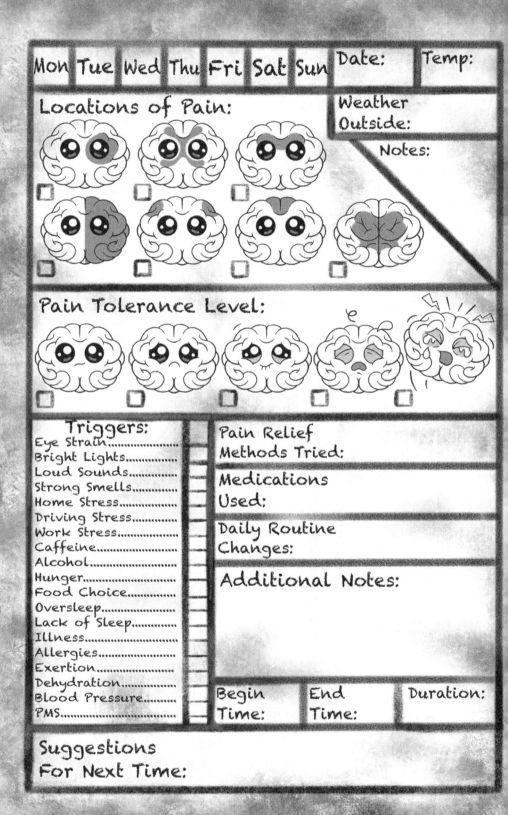

| Mon | Tue | Wed | Thu | Fri | Sat | Sun | Date: | Temp: |

Locations of Pain:

Weather Outside:

Notes:

Pain Tolerance Level:

Triggers:

Eye Strain..........................
Bright Lights.....................
Loud Sounds.....................
Strong Smells...................
Home Stress......................
Driving Stress...................
Work Stress......................
Caffeine.............................
Alcohol...............................
Hunger...............................
Food Choice.....................
Oversleep...........................
Lack of Sleep...................
Illness................................
Allergies.............................
Exertion.............................
Dehydration.....................
Blood Pressure................
PMS....................................

Pain Relief Methods Tried:

Medications Used:

Daily Routine Changes:

Additional Notes:

Begin Time:

End Time:

Duration:

Suggestions For Next Time:

Mon	Tue	Wed	Thu	Fri	Sat	Sun	Date:	Temp:

Locations of Pain:

Weather Outside:

Notes:

Pain Tolerance Level:

Triggers:

Eye Strain................
Bright Lights..............
Loud Sounds............
Strong Smells............
Home Stress..............
Driving Stress..........
Work Stress..............
Caffeine....................
Alcohol.....................
Hunger......................
Food Choice.............
Oversleep.................
Lack of Sleep............
Illness......................
Allergies...................
Exertion...................
Dehydration.............
Blood Pressure..........
PMS.........................

Pain Relief Methods Tried:

Medications Used:

Daily Routine Changes:

Additional Notes:

Begin Time:	End Time:	Duration:

Suggestions For Next Time:

| Mon | Tue | Wed | Thu | Fri | Sat | Sun | Date: | Temp: |

Locations of Pain:

Weather
Outside:

Notes:

☐ ☐ ☐

☐ ☐ ☐ ☐

Pain Tolerance Level:

☐ ☐ ☐ ☐ ☐

Triggers:

Eye Strain.................
Bright Lights.............
Loud Sounds.............
Strong Smells...........
Home Stress............
Driving Stress..........
Work Stress.............
Caffeine...................
Alcohol....................
Hunger.....................
Food Choice............
Oversleep................
Lack of Sleep...........
Illness.....................
Allergies..................
Exertion...................
Dehydration.............
Blood Pressure.........
PMS.........................

**Pain Relief
Methods Tried:**

**Medications
Used:**

**Daily Routine
Changes:**

Additional Notes:

| Begin Time: | End Time: | Duration: |

**Suggestions
For Next Time:**

| Mon | Tue | Wed | Thu | Fri | Sat | Sun | Date: | Temp: |

Locations of Pain:

Weather
Outside:

Notes:

Pain Tolerance Level:

Triggers:

Eye Strain.....................
Bright Lights................
Loud Sounds................
Strong Smells...............
Home Stress.................
Driving Stress...............
Work Stress..................
Caffeine........................
Alcohol.........................
Hunger.........................
Food Choice.................
Oversleep......................
Lack of Sleep...............
Illness...........................
Allergies.......................
Exertion........................
Dehydration.................
Blood Pressure............
PMS..............................

Pain Relief
Methods Tried:

Medications
Used:

Daily Routine
Changes:

Additional Notes:

Begin
Time:

End
Time:

Duration:

Suggestions
For Next Time:

Mon | Tue | Wed | Thu | Fri | Sat | Sun | Date: | Temp:

Locations of Pain:

Weather Outside:

Notes:

Pain Tolerance Level:

Triggers:
Eye Strain..................
Bright Lights..............
Loud Sounds...............
Strong Smells.............
Home Stress................
Driving Stress.............
Work Stress.................
Caffeine.....................
Alcohol.....................
Hunger.......................
Food Choice...............
Oversleep...................
Lack of Sleep..............
Illness.......................
Allergies....................
Exertion....................
Dehydration...............
Blood Pressure...........
PMS..........................

Pain Relief Methods Tried:

Medications Used:

Daily Routine Changes:

Additional Notes:

Begin Time: | End Time: | Duration:

Suggestions For Next Time:

| Mon | Tue | Wed | Thu | Fri | Sat | Sun | Date: | Temp: |

Locations of Pain:

Weather Outside:

Notes:

Pain Tolerance Level:

Triggers:
Eye Strain..................
Bright Lights..............
Loud Sounds...............
Strong Smells............
Home Stress...............
Driving Stress............
Work Stress...............
Caffeine....................
Alcohol.....................
Hunger......................
Food Choice..............
Oversleep..................
Lack of Sleep............
Illness......................
Allergies...................
Exertion....................
Dehydration..............
Blood Pressure..........
PMS..........................

Pain Relief Methods Tried:

Medications Used:

Daily Routine Changes:

Additional Notes:

| Begin Time: | End Time: | Duration: |

Suggestions For Next Time:

| Mon | Tue | Wed | Thu | Fri | Sat | Sun | Date: | Temp: |

Locations of Pain:

☐   ☐   ☐

☐   ☐   ☐   ☐

Weather
Outside:

Notes:

Pain Tolerance Level:

☐   ☐   ☐   ☐   ☐

Triggers:

Eye Strain.................
Bright Lights.............
Loud Sounds.............
Strong Smells...........
Home Stress.............
Driving Stress...........
Work Stress..............
Caffeine....................
Alcohol.....................
Hunger......................
Food Choice.............
Oversleep..................
Lack of Sleep............
Illness......................
Allergies...................
Exertion....................
Dehydration..............
Blood Pressure..........
PMS..........................

Pain Relief
Methods Tried:

Medications
Used:

Daily Routine
Changes:

Additional Notes:

| Begin Time: | End Time: | Duration: |

Suggestions
For Next Time:

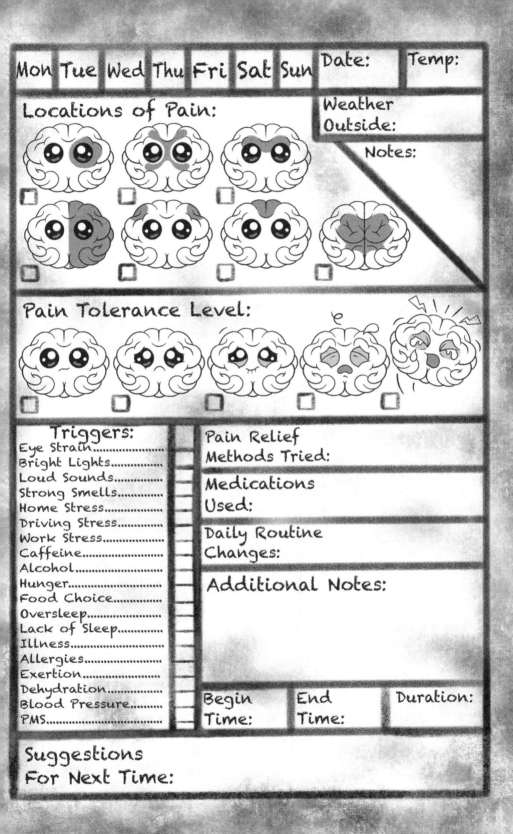

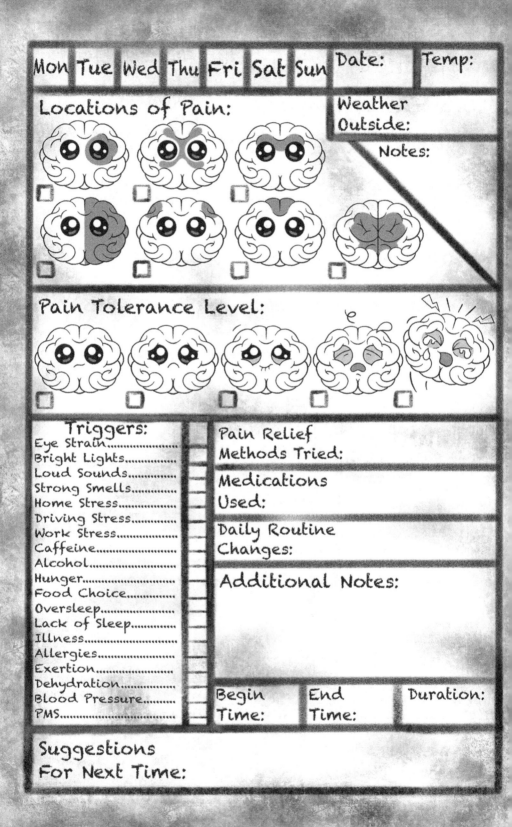

Mon | Tue | Wed | Thu | Fri | Sat | Sun | Date: | Temp:

Locations of Pain:

Weather Outside:

Notes:

Pain Tolerance Level:

Triggers:
Eye Strain..................
Bright Lights...............
Loud Sounds...............
Strong Smells.............
Home Stress................
Driving Stress.............
Work Stress................
Caffeine.....................
Alcohol.......................
Hunger.......................
Food Choice...............
Oversleep...................
Lack of Sleep.............
Illness........................
Allergies.....................
Exertion.....................
Dehydration...............
Blood Pressure..........
PMS...........................

Pain Relief
Methods Tried:

Medications
Used:

Daily Routine
Changes:

Additional Notes:

Begin
Time:

End
Time:

Duration:

Suggestions
For Next Time: